KIMBALL / THE POCKET GUIDE TO

LONDON THEATRE

WITH A FOREWORD BY SIR PETER HALL

Xanadu

Acknowledgements

Barry Turner and Mary Fulton, *The Playgoer's Companion*.
Frank Cook, *The London Theatre Scene*.
Christopher Brereton *et al*, *Curtains!!!*
John Russel Taylor, *The Penguin Dictionary of the Theatre*.
Peter Roberts, *Theatre in Britain*.
Michael Billington, *The Guinness Book of Theatre Facts and Feats*.
Mander and Mitchenson, *Theatres of London*.
Mander and Mitchenson, *Lost Theatres of London*.
Phyllis Hartnoll (ed.) *The Concise Oxford Companion to the Theatre*.
British Theatre Directory.
British Alternative Theatre Directory.
The Reader's Encyclopedia.
The Complete Guide to Britain's National Theatre.

The publisher would like to thank London Regional Transport (Underground Map Registered user No. 87/644) and all those theatres which contributed seating plans and illustrations.

Map by courtesy of the Society of West End Theatre © 1987

Special thanks to Miss Sue Ellsworth, the author's tireless and unflappable research assistant, without whose help this book could not have been produced.

British Library Cataloguing in Publication Data

Kimball, George
    The pocket guide to London theatre.
    1. London (England)—Theatres 2. London (England—
    Description—1951— Guidebooks
    I. Title
    792'.09421   PN2596.L6

    ISBN 0-947761-12-8

Copyright © George Kimball 1987

Published by Xanadu Publications Limited
5 Uplands Road, Hornsey, London N8 9NN

Set by Digatype Limited, London

Printed and bound in Spain

FOREWORD

by Sir Peter Hall

I think the record since the war in British theatre is second to none. No other country has twenty-five world-ranking dramatists for a start. And without question it has been a great age of British acting.

One reason certainly for our success is that the British have always had a genius for theatre, partly perhaps because we are a basically puritanical and inhibited yet also a violently emotional, eccentric people; it's a powerful duality. From that too comes our passion for debating the theatre. There are few countries where the theatre is as closely watched and argued about as it is here.

The theatre in Britain has rightly, as well, taken on the responsibility of being a place where society can debate with itself the live issues of the day. When you have had a good evening in the theatre, whether you laugh or cry, you walk out slightly changed, slightly challenged, thinking about the nature of your own life.

But the main reason for the extraordinary flowering of drama in Britain since the war is the introduction of government subsidy. By the 1950s the cost of putting on a play — a labour intensive, hand-made object — had become so great that the future of our theatre seemed in jeopardy. Then, just at the right moment, subsidy came from government, and bred a host of new stars.

The great post-war figures had of course already established themselves before 1940: Olivier, Ashcroft, Richardson, Gielgud, Guinness, Redgrave. But in the 'Fifties and 'Sixties came Scofield, Tutin, Joan Plowright, Finney, Bates, Judi Dench, Tom Courtenay, Hopkins, Maggie Smith, Glenda Jackson, Ian McKellan. New playrights made their appearance, too: Pinter, Osborne, Wesker, Bolt, Bond, Stoppard. And new directors arrived: Tony Richardson, Brook, Joan Littlewood, John Dexter, Trevor Nunn, Terry Hands, Lindsay Anderson, William Gaskill, John Barton. It was the new subsidies that not only enabled all these dazzling talents to succeed, but reminded us that the theatre, historically, has nearly always been subsidised by somebody — the king or the state or the religion of the day. Governments of whatever party recognized that fact in the 1950s and 'sixties.

Then in the late 'seventies the official attitude towards subsidy changed. A new government decided that private sponsorship was the answer and that government subsidies should, in real terms, be reduced. As it turns out they were wrong.

Fifteen years ago, for example, the Royal Court — probably the most important theatre in Britain for the staging of new works — produced 17 or 18 plays a season. Now it does six. When a dramatist sits down at his typewriter today he automatically thinks, 'I'd be a fool to try anything with more than six characters and one set because so few managements can pay to put it on.'

There isn't at present a subsidized theatre anywhere in the country that can afford to work at full stretch. It's almost impossible for our children to see Shakespeare performed outside London today because so few repertory companies can afford to produce his plays — or indeed any other large-cast classics. And all of this rebounds on Britain's commercial theatre. The fewer new plays that can be produced, the fewer new actors, directors and writers that are able to develop, the less potentially profitable is the material the commercial theatre has available to draw upon.

Yet despite its current difficulties, the resilient British theatre has managed so far to hold on to its great reputation. We still have two major subsidized theatres, the RSC and the National, working in creative competition. We still have marvellous repertory companies all over the land. We currently have over 40 commercial theatres operating in the West End alone. And we have a fringe theatre unmatched anywhere for its vitality.

There is a great deal of muddled thinking in all political parties about the value of the arts to this country. The Right maintains that if the arts need subsidy then they must be losing money — whereas in fact they earn for the country far, far more than they cost. The Left seems to have the idea that art of high quality is elitist and therefore suspect, which is a curious conclusion. So neither is right in my view. Our task is to prove it by shooting our mouths off from time to time, and by doing all we can to keep the traditions of the British theatre thriving.

CONTENTS

SECTION I
THE LONDON THEATRE WORLD
PAGE 6

I THE LONDON THEATRE WORLD

Which way to Drury Lane,
Which way to Wyndham's?
—old London lament

London, the richest and most exciting theatre town in the English-speaking world, can also be one of the most frustrating if you don't know your way around it pretty thoroughly. The purpose of this guide is simply to help more people enjoy more plays by making theatregoing in London as straightforward and as snag-proof as is humanly possible. It will also help you to avoid paying more than you have to: always a good idea.

This first section of the guide provides all the essential information about how to find out what's playing at the London theatres each week, how to choose, book and pay for seats, the most direct way to get to each theatre, and what to expect when you finally arrive. Following this are listings of children's theatres, student theatres, alternative cabarets, concert halls and theatre ticket agencies.

Section II contains detailed information about each of the 90 or so mainstream and fringe theatres currently operating full-time in London. The theatres are listed alphabetically, for easy reference. Individual theatre entries include mailing addresses and important telephone numbers, seating plans, production policies, auditorium and stage designs, practical facilities (including those for the disabled), schedules of performances, booking procedures, price ranges, reduced-price concessions, theatre amenities and extra-theatrical activities. Each entry also contains a brief history of the theatre in question, full information about how to reach it by bus, underground or train, and even step-by-step directions from public transport stops to the theatre entrance.

Section III is a glossary of theatre and theatrical terms, and for convenience all the maps are positioned at the end of the book.

It's a great deal of information to pack into one small volume, but we honestly believe that we have managed to include practically everything that you will need to know about the labyrinthine mysteries of the London theatre world. So the next time you find yourself with only ten minutes to go, the tickets still uncollected and the theatre nowhere in sight, simply reach into your pocket—and then enjoy a marvellous evening out, with our blessings.

What's playing

Note The term 'West End', which properly refers to London's central theatre district, is also used colloquially to describe any stage production which is either traditional in character or, in a somewhat pejorative sense, commercial. Theatres located outside the West End which regularly stage such productions are also frequently referred to as West End theatres. To avoid confusion here, 'West End' is only used in reference to the theatre district itself. In all other contexts 'mainstream' is the term employed.

Most London daily newspapers—notably the *Standard*, *Times*, *Guardian* and *Independant*—provide up-to-date information about what's playing in the West End and at the larger mainstream and fringe theatres around London. The *Sunday Times* and *Observer* also offer extensive theatre listings plus regular reviews by London's leading critics. But for full, accurate coverage of the entire theatre scene, the most useful and readily-obtainable sources of information are the weekly magazines *Time Out* and *What's On and Where to Go in London*.

Time Out Published every Thursday and available from all newsagents at 80 pence, it offers a complete listing of every mainstream and fringe show playing in London each week, plus short reviews of newly-opened plays and a quite substantial 'recommended' section. Listings are presented alphabetically by theatre name, with fringe, lunchtime and other alternative productions given first under the heading 'Fringe Shows' and mainstream productions, wherever located, given next under the heading 'West End'. Once somewhere to the left of Che Guevara in its editorial attitudes, *Time Out* has mellowed in recent years and now tailors its reviews and recommendations to a fairly wide range of theatrical tastes. It may still be wise to seek second critical opinions about new or unfamiliar shows, but the magazine is notoriously conscientious about its facts and can always be relied upon for accurate, up-to-date information about venues, prices, curtain times, weekly schedules, opening and closing dates, coming attractions, and (most helpful) last-minute changes and misadventures. *City Limits* contains very similar information for those of more left-wing dispositions.

What's On And Where To Go In London Also published on Thursdays and available from all newsagents at 50 pence, this offers an omnibus theatre section called 'On Stage' in which productions are grouped into sometimes faintly confusing categories—'Straight Plays', 'Musicals and Comedies', 'Thrillers', 'Fringe' etc.—and then listed alphabetically by play title. Longish reviews are scattered throughout the section, and perhaps because the magazine is angled more toward out-of-town vistors the editorial tone tends to be fairly neutral. Again, coverage of the London theatre scene is comprehensive, and all facts are accurately presented and up-to-date. There is also an out-of-town listing for larger theatres within about 100 miles of London. Also of interest to theatre-goers seeking more detailed information about London and regional theatre are:

Plays and Players Published monthly at £1.25 and available from most central London newsagents and from larger newsagents in outlying districts. One of London's oldest and most respected theatre journals, **Plays and Players** offers reviews, profiles, interviews, listings and editorial articles in a handsomely produced, well-written package for both casual and inveterate theatre-goers.

The Stage London's 'official' live-entertainment trade paper is published weekly and available from most newsagents at 30 pence. Reviews, features, editorials, facts and figures are all presented in a snappily professional show-biz style, and for those with a taste for inside information there are news items covering every aspect of the business from Lord Olivier's latest honour to the current whereabouts of The Adorable Dancing White Rabbit.

Choosing theatre seats

Prices Generally speaking, the less you spend for theatre tickets the further away from the stage and the higher up in the auditorium you will find yourself. Stalls (US orchestra) are normally the most expensive seats, diminishing slightly in price as one moves toward the back of the theatre. Seats at the front of the dress (first) circle usually cost the same or slightly less than best stalls seats, again gradually diminishing in price as one moves toward the back of the circle. Price continues to drop as one moves up the theatre circle by circle until the least expensive seats are finally encountered at the top of the balcony, familiarly called 'The Gods' because you're right up there with 'em (literally so in many of London's fine old Victorian theatres where ceiling and cornice decorations feature huge *trompe l'oeil* scenes of Olympian grandeur together with gangs of splendidly ornate plaster-and-gilt deities disporting themselves in theatre 'heaven'). Prices may also go down in any given seating section the further you move toward one or the other of its ends. These pricing rules hold generally for both traditionally designed theatres and for more modern ones with open plan auditoriums. There are two exceptions, however: (1) In most traditionally designed theatres, seats at the very front of the stalls – those nearest the stage and usually some distance below stage level – will be less expensive than those a few rows further back. (2) For certain grand productions mounted in the largest London theatres, several rows of seats may be arranged on stage around the back. These will cost even less than seats in the farthest reaches of The Gods. But there is usually a hitch: along with seeing every thing from behind and being denied the full effect of the stage set, you may suddenly be handed a spear or similar prop and pressed into service for a crowd scene. An exciting prospect for closet hams, perhaps, but otherwise not.

Price ranges do vary from one theatre to another according to size, location, and the kind of show being staged. The more lavish mainstream musicals will cost a good deal wherever you sit. But considering today's skyrocketing production costs and the stinginess of the grants currently being offered to the subsidized theatre section by a supposedly arts-supportive government, it is amazing how little you do need to spend to enjoy an evening in the London theatre. In most mainstream theatres, seats in the stalls or lower circles can still be purchased for around £10. Balcony seats rarely cost more than £5. And in most fringe theatres, where seats are usually one-price and unreserved, you can have the best seat in the house, providing you arrive early enough to claim it, for as little as £3.

View Assuming price is no object and you like viewing plays more or less head-on, choose seats in the middle or back stalls. If you actually like looking up at the stage, take seats in the front. Remember that in side stalls, though they may cost a bit less, the further forward you sit the more restricted your view of the action will be—especially in smaller, traditionally designed theatres with proscenium stages.

If you prefer looking slightly down onto the stage, as I do (I like the over-all effect and the chance to spot little things going on at the back), take seats in the circle. Angled views from the circle's extremities usually present no special viewing problems except again in smaller, traditionally designed theatres where the near side of the proscenium arch can sometimes cut off a portion of the stage.

Balcony seats (in some theatres called rather more grandly 'upper circles' or 'galleries', but balconies nonetheless) offer the same viewing advantages and drawbacks as circle seats, only a bit more so and with one important exception: in smaller, traditionally designed theatres, the balcony's steep rake can produce serious states of alarm in vertigo sufferers. I once heard of a vertiginous girl who, as a student unable to afford better than The Gods, actually had to tie herself to her seat arm with a scarf before she felt secure enough to become lost in the action below. So be warned: if heights do make you dizzy, avoid balconies, especially in smaller West End theatres.

Box seats, unless located at ridiculously oblique angles to the stage (as some are in some West End theatres), offer roughly the same view as do circle seats and are, of course, wonderfully comfortable. Some commentators, perhaps on political grounds, tend to be rather disdainful of boxes.

Personally, I can't think of a more agreeable place from which to watch a play so long as the angle of view is reasonable and memory of the cost doesn't diminish your pleasure in the performance. (In fact, a box seat usually costs only a pound or so more than a seat in the middle stalls or front of the first circle).

Audibility In most of the older, traditionally designed theatres, the best places to hear from are the front and middle stalls, the lower circles and the boxes. Up in The Gods it requires concentration to understand all that's being said on stage, particularly in winter when an inordinate amount of coughing invariably goes on all over the auditorium. Another place in older theatres where hearing can be a problem is at the very back of the stalls beneath the overhang of the first circle. Where circles extend well out, diminished audibility can be a real nuisance – something to watch out for when considering the price of stalls seats.

In most modern theatres, with their open plan auditoriums and careful acoustical engineering, audibility tends to be uniformly good in all parts of the hall. It is very often the case, in fact, that the higher up one sits the better one hears. Acoustical quality, however, sometimes suffers from the lack of heavy fabrics and complicated decorative elements found in older theatres.

Fringe theatres tend to vary so widely in design that little can be said generally about their audibility or, indeed, about their viewing characteristics. Most are fairly small, however, which means that audibility and viewing are both quite good; and in some of the newer, purpose-built fringe theatres both are excellent.

Booking seats

In person You may book seats in person at the theatre box office, normally between 10am and 8pm Monday through Saturday. (Box office hours and days will be noted in individual theatre entries in Section II). Most theatre box offices sell tickets for current and future productions, though a few of the largest theatres have advance box offices where they will ask you to book for future productions and even for future performances of a current production. Payment may be made by cash, cheque (British only), or credit card. (Individual theatre entries in Section II list which credit cards are accepted.) Booking in person allows you to look at a full-size seating plan of the theatre and to chose seats by section, row and number. It also gives you a chance to locate the theatre if you don't already know it. But there is one drawback: if the show you want to see is very popular, you may arrive at the box office only to be told it's sold out—and will be for the next six weeks or even months. That doesn't mean it *is* sold out; only that you will have to try the ticket agencies, or, if you're feeling lucky, turn up an hour before curtain time and queue for standby tickets. (See below for details.)

Telephone booking You may book seats by telephone through the box office at any time during box office hours. Don't however, expect a prompt answer—or any answer at all—if you ring within a half hour of curtain time. That's when the staff are at their busiest. Some theatres permit telephone booking by section, row and number, others by section (or price range) only. But it's always worth asking. Many theatres require advance telephone bookings to be paid at least three working days before the date of the performance. Bookings made less than three days before the performance must be collected at the box office at least one hour before curtain time. Other theatres require telephone bookings to be paid within 3-4 days of being made (see Section II for details). Payment may be by cash, cheque or credit card if you collect tickets in person. Telephone bookings may also be paid by post with a cheque, money order or (frequently) your credit card number and full permanent address. Tickets will be held at the box office for collection, or sent to you if you include a stamped addressed envelope with your postal payment. Telephone bookings not paid on time will go on standby sale approximately 1 hour before curtain time.

Postal booking You may book seats by writing to the theatre box office stating the name of the show you want to see, the date you wish to attend (with at *least* one alternative date), whether matinee or evening performance, the number of tickets required, and the preferred seating section (or price range). Include a SAE and a signed cheque made out to the theatre with the amount left blank and an initialed note at the top stating 'no more than ...' and the maximum you plan to spend for the tickets. Staff will complete the cheque or, if your request can't be met, return it to you. If you wish, you may collect tickets booked and paid for by post at the box office anytime before the performance begins, but make certain ahead of time that your booking is confirmed.

Credit card booking Most mainstream and many fringe theatres provide separate phone lines for credit card booking. Hours usually correspond to box office hours, but a few theatres run 24-hour 7-day-week credit card telephone booking services. (See individual theatres in Section II.) Seat choice is normally by section or price range only, but again it's worth asking. Confirmation is immediate, so tickets may be collected at the box office anytime before the curtain. In theatres where separate phone lines are not provided, telephone credit card booking can often be made through the box office.

Ticket agency booking There are scores of theatre ticket agencies located all over central London and the outer districts. Most handle only top price seats and many charge a service fee of 15-20 per cent, but mainstream theatres, particularly in the West End, assign up to 30 per cent of their tickets to agencies, and they are frequently the only source of so-called 'unobtainables'. When faced with 'sell outs', therefore, or if you simply want to avoid the trouble of other booking methods, agencies are the answer. All agencies accept telephone and telephone credit card bookings, many offer same-day delivery service of tickets in greater London, nearly all can set up theatre-dinner (-hotel, -weekend) packages, and a few even provide credit facilities. (see page 18 for a selected list of theatre ticket agencies in London.)

Subscription booking Virtually all of the larger repertory theatres in London, whether mainstream or fringe, offer advance postal booking schemes to sub-scription members. For an annual fee of a few pounds you can subscribe to a theatre's mailing list and receive information about future productions plus postal booking forms. Seating choice is normally limited to section or price range only, but the chance to book well in advance nearly always guarantees getting the seats you want, and many theatres offer discounts to their members. Non-repertory theatres, (e.g. most in the West End), do not offer such schemes simply because they never know how long a given production will run. (If, for example, in 1952 the Ambassadors theatre had offered advance postal booking for its next production, subscribers would have had to wait 22 years before Agatha Christie's *The Mousetrap* finally transferred to the St Martin's next door. And hypothetical St Martin's subscribers would *still* be waiting for their next play to come on, *The Mousetrap* having now run continuously for some 33 years!)

Reduced price concessions
Virtually all London theatres, save the two or three blessed each year with season-long sell-outs, offer concessions on seat prices in at least one of the following ways:

Preview nights Usually a large percentage off all seats for final run-through performances held during the week or so immediately preceding a show's press premiere and first night. Actors generally beg you not to attend previews, which are, in effect, full dress rehearsals staged before paying audiences without benefit of 'retakes' when the star goes up in his lines or the door that's supposed to burst open doesn't. In fact, previews are usually okay, if seldom brilliant, and certainly better than not seeing a show at all if it happens to be booked solid after opening.

Press night One or two evening performances staged for the benefit of the theatre critics immediately prior to a show's opening night. Some reduction on all seats for the public (whose reactions the critics like to study), and the rather exciting experience of watching a play in the company of several score-hungry sharks.

Weekday and Saturday matinées All theatres take at least a pound off the price of all seats for their afternoon performances, the reason being that they often aren't as sharp as evening ones. The company is still recuperating from the previous night's work, and actors don't relate very well to daylight, anyway. Given the choice, evening performances are usually a better bet.

Groups Nearly all larger theatres take a pound or so off of their higher-priced tickets for group bookings of (approximately) 12 or more people. Some theatres also offer reduced prices on less expensive seats for student groups and club bookings.

Special categories Virtually all theatres offer special reductions on some or all seats to the following: old-age pensioners (OAPs), disabled, registered unemployed, under-24 British Railcard holders, students, members of the theatrical union Equity, Musician's union, and NATTKE. Reductions in some categories will be for standby tickets only, and credentials proving qualification for reductions must be shown.

Theatre/British Rail Package for theatre-goers travelling into London on British Rail, a travel reduction is offered when combined with a West End ticket. For details write to: Theatre and Concert Rail Club, P.O. Box 1, St. Albans, Herts. Telephone: St. Albans 34457.

Theatre/dinner packages Many West End theatres offer a combined theatre ticket and dinner scheme in co-operation with local restaurants which may be booked at the time of reserving tickets. The reduction amounts to about 10%, and if you do plan to dine out before or after the theatre the convenience of having your table already booked is a real blessing.

SWET ticket booth The Society of West End Theatres operates a ticket booth in Leicester Square (see West End map, end of book) where tickets for most West End productions may be purchased, in person only, first come first served, for half price plus 75 pence service charge on the day of the show. Cash payment only, four tickets maximum per customer. Open from 12 noon for matinées and from 12.30 pm to 6.30pm for evening performances.

Fringe box office Located in the foyer of the Duke of York's Theatre, St Martin's Lane. Telephone (01) 379 6002 for information, advance booking, credit card booking. Many of the central and outer London fringe theatres sell tickets and offer reduced-price schemes through the Duke of York's box office, open 10am-6pm every day except Sunday.

Getting to the theatre

London boasts one of the most reliable, comprehensive and resonably-priced public transport systems of any city its size in the world. No London theatre is more than a few minutes' walk from a bus, underground or British Rail stop, and the system itself is about as easy to manage as any you will ever encounter—until, that is, you have to get off it and start looking for your theatre. I can still remember an evening last summer when, riding up Charing Cross Road aboard a bus on my way to review a film, I heard a baffled American couple being given three different sets of wrong directions to a theatre which was, at that very moment, actually visible between buildings less than 50 yards away. All of the direction-givers were Londoners, all were trying their best to help, all believed sincerely that they knew where that theatre was, and all were wrong. The moral of that little story is, any tourist map which provides nothing but lists of bus numbers and then expects you to complete your journey with the assistance of well-meaning strangers in the street is going to cause you to miss a lot of first-act curtains. So:

At the end of the book you will find a complete map of London's Underground System, plus a map of London's most concentrated theatre area, showing where the theatres are in relation to the tube stops. The walking directions found under 'Getting There' in individual theatre entries will take you straight to your destination. Remember, however, that London is a huge city, and to make your way around it efficiently you will need: (1) A London street atlas (I recommend the *Nicholson London Streetfinder*, sold at newsagents and bookshops everywhere, and noticeably easier to read than its somewhat better-known rival the *London A-Z*). (2) A London-Wide Bus Map, available free from the headquarters of London Transport, 55 Broadway SW1, (telephone (01) 222 1234 and they'll send you one), or obtainable in person from London Transport information centres located at Victoria Station, Euston Station, Charing Cross Station, King's Cross Station, Piccadilly Circus underground, Oxford Circus underground, St. James's Park underground, and Heathrow Airport.

Bus If travelling to the theatre by bus, consult 'Getting There' buses in your theatre's individual entry in Section II to discover which number and stop you want. Then use the walking directions for that stop, to get you to the theatre.

Regular London buses run daily (unless otherwise noted) from about 6am until 11.00 or 11.30pm. There is also a network of all-night buses (designated 'N') which serve key London locations nightly (unless otherwise noted) from about 11.30pm until about 6.00am. To be on the safe side allow 10 minutes for every mile you must travel plus another 10-15 minutes' wait at the bus stop. (Much longer waiting periods operate between night buses, but you'll find times for these on the bus stops.) You may arrive early, but unless something unusual happens you're sure not to be late. (Note: Make especially generous time allowances for any bus that runs the length of Oxford Street or Piccadilly. The habitual traffic jams, particularly during tourist seasons, can be diabolical.)

Underground If travelling to the theatre by 'tube', consult 'Getting There, Underground' in your theatre's Section II entry and then proceed as for buses using the underground map at the front of the book and the walking directions for your underground stop.

The underground system operates from about 6am until just after 11pm. Trains do sometimes appear as late as 11.30pm, but not always, so judge your time accordingly—and remember there is no all-night system. Allow approximately 5 minutes for every stop you must travel, plus again a 10-15 minute wait at the station.

British Rail If you are travelling to the theatre by rail from outside London you will, of course, arrive at one of the city's main railway stations. To make your way from there to your theatre, simply follow the steps outlined above for travelling by bus or underground (whichever is most convenient). But note that scores of theatres are within walking distance of Charing Cross Station, and a few within walking distance of other main stations. So first look up your theatre in Section II and consult 'Getting There, British Rail' before bothering about bus or underground connections.

British Rail also operates a Greater London and Districts train service which connects outlying stations with a number of centrally located main and district stations. Your station of departure should provide you with all relevant information, and you will then find walking directions to theatres noted under 'Getting There' British Rail in Section II theatre entries.

Car parks If driving your own car to the theatre, particularly in the West End, you may have to use a public car park unless you are lucky enough to find street parking. (Street parking on single yellow lines is permitted after 6.30pm Monday-Friday, and after 1pm on Saturdays unless otherwise noted). Note that many West End theatres offer a discount on parking in specified lots and garages with the purchase of a ticket. Check on this when you book.

Taxis If you want to book a taxi to take you to the theatre or collect you afterwards, phone Dial-A-Cab on (01) 253 5000 or Radio-Taxis on (01) 263 9496 and they will make the arrangements. Dial-A-Cab and Radio-Taxi drivers and cars are licensed by the London police and subject to all regulations governing normal London cab operation. So long as your journey is not more than six miles and confined to the Greater London area, the charges cannot exceed those shown on the meter. Charges for longer journeys should be settled at time of booking.

If you want to telephone a licensed taxi rank use the following numbers:

Central London	606 4526
North London	837 2394
South East London	703 4851
South West London	589 5242 (South Kensington)
	730 2664 (Chelsea)
	834 1014 (Westminister)
West London	723 9907 (Bayswater & Paddington)
	937 0736 (Kensington)
	286 2566 (Maida Vale & Notting Hill)

Mini-cabs (private, unlicensed taxis) may be contacted using numbers listed in the London yellow pages. Often less expensive for journeys of more than six miles. Charges should be settled at time of booking.

Theatre amenities and facilities

Food Many London theatres, particularly the newer ones, now incorporate buffet restaurants or snack bars where hot dishes, sandwiches, salads, desserts, soft drinks, beer and wine are on sale from anywhere up to 1½ hours before evening perfomances begin. Some buffets and snack bars also open for lunch on matinée days. A few large theatres also incorporate full-scale restaurants where tables may be booked and meals enjoyed from about 1½ hours before curtain time. Fringe theatres located in larger arts or community centres, or in pubs, normally share restaurant and buffet facilities with the main premises; and of course lunchtime and supper theatres include lunch or supper in the price of the ticket. But all London theatres, even those without other eating facilities, at least sell ice cream and other snacks during the interval.

Drink All London theatres incorporate at least one licensed bar where a full range of drinks is available from about an hour before the evening performance begins until the end of the interval. (Drinks cannot be sold during matinées because of English licensing laws). In some larger theatres, bars also remain open after evening performances. And in all theatres you may order and pay for intermission drinks before the performance begins in order to avoid the scrum at the bar which invariably commences 30 seconds after the first-act curtain falls.

Disabled facilities Most London theatres provide special seating accommodation for disabled people confined to wheelchairs. Most theatres now also provide induction loop systems for the hard of hearing. Many of the newer theatres incorporate specially equipped restrooms for disabled persons, as well as elevators or wheelchair ramps to upper seating levels. When booking seats, always mention any disabled person, or persons, in your party so that special arrangements, if required, can be made in advance.

Extra-theatrical activities and facilities Many of the newer theatres, particularly subsidized and fringe theatres, or those located in community or arts complexes, now offer a wide variety of extra-theatrical activities and facilities on their premises including music recitals, art or craft exhibitions, book shops, record stalls, space for meetings or workshop activities, and even cinemas, all of which are noted in individual theatre entries in Section II.

Hints, advice, warnings

The following bits of information are meant largely for novice London theatregoers. They are presented in no particular order, some are quite important, some less so, but all are aimed at saving you either time, discomfort, or both, and therefore probably worth taking a moment to look at.

● For tax purposes, many London fringe theatres operate in principle as private clubs rather than public theatres and therefore require new patrons to take out 'membership' (usually around 50 pence) ½ hour before a performance. Membership is usually eternal, (though in a few cases only annual), and most fringe theatres have a reciprocal arrangement whereby membership in one serves as membership in all.

● If you like watching a play through binoculars, bring your own. The ones in West End theatres that pop out of little boxes when coins are inserted have not been cleaned or adjusted since they were first installed during the reign of Edward VII.

● When a theatre advertises itself as being 'air-conditioned', the term can mean anything from real air-conditioning to a window left open in the loft. It usually means some kind of fan extractor system, which only partially freshens the air without cooling it, so be prepared. Dress lightly on hot summer days unless you know its the real thing. (Notes on individual theatres in Section II will help), and stay out of balconies if stuffy, overheated air makes you giddy.

● Theatre heating in winter is quite another matter, and can only be described as ferocious—unless it doesn't work at all. It usually does though, and since 70°-75° Farenheit is the norm—certainly in the West End—light clothing is again recommended.

● As for clothing generally, you needn't dress up at all to go to the London theatre if you don't feel like it. People really don't care what you wear—England is a democracy—so think of comfort first.

● I've said this only a couple of pages ago, but it's worth repeating: if you want a drink during the interval, order it before the performance begins. Intervals are short and it's no fun spending all of it in a mob at the bar waiting to order a drink which invariably arrives just as the warning bell rings.

● The casts of London productions change from time to time. Notice is always published, but if you miss seeing it you may also miss a favourite actor or actress whose performance you particularly wanted to watch. So when you book tickets check to be sure that certain members of the cast haven't recently been replaced.

● If you arrive late at the theatre, be prepared to wait until the first scene break, or even the end of the first act, before being allowed to take your seat. English democracy in the theatre does not extend to disturbances caused by late-comers.

● If you are going to see a play at the Barbican for the first time, allow a minimum of 15 minutes extra to find *anything*.

● Steer clear of touts bearing gifts in the form of impossible-to-get theatre tickets. The 'gifts' will cost several times what they should; and while there are certainly honest touts hustling legitimate tickets around the West End, there are also unscrupulous ones selling worthless fakes. The problem is, you can't tell the real thing from the fraud—tout or ticket.

Theatre ticket agencies

ABBEY BOX OFFICE
27 Victoria Street SW1   222 2992/222 3231/222 4261
Central Booking Hall, Victoria Station (opposite platform 13) 828 6902

ACE TICKETS—DAVID BROWN ASSOCIATES
43 Lavender Hill SW11 5QW   223 8173/228 0093

CITY ENTERTAINMENTS
39 Marylebone Lane W1   388 5353/388 0629

DIAL-A-TICKET
30 Craven Street, Strand WC2   930 8331/930 8332

FENCHURCH BOOKING AGENCY
3 London Street EC3
709 0671/928 8585 (theatre tickets)
95 Southwark Street SE1   633 9551

FIRST CALL
Telephone booking by credit card on 240 7200 (100 lines). Open 24 hours, seven days per week.

GROUP SALES BOX OFFICE
Norris House, Norris Street SW1   930 6123

KEITH PROWSE & CO

Ticket Shops
Plantation House, Fenchurch Street EC3   626 2784
27a Shaftesbury Avenue W1 734 7331
44 Shaftesbury Avenue W1 437 8976
1 Melcombe Street NW1 935 5415
5 Grosvenor Street W1 629 4775
27 Throgmorton Street EC2 588 0171

Stores
Bentalls: Wood Street, Kingston-upon Thames, Surrey
546 1001
Harrods: Knightsbridge SW1 589 1101/589 1102
Selfridges: Oxford Street W1 629 1234 ext. 3710
Virgin Megastore: 30 Oxford Street W1 631 1234

Hotels
Browns Hotel: Dover Street W1 493 6020
Claridges Hotel: Brook Street W1 493 0130
Grosvenor House Hotel: Park Lane W1 493 0364
Inn On The Park: Hamilton Place W1   499 1842
Inter-Continental Hotel: Park Lane W1 491 2884
Mayfair Hotel: Stratton Street W1 493 9979
Mount Royal Hotel: Marble Arch W1 493 0497
Park Lane Hotel: Piccadilly W1   493 0823
Regent Palace Hotel: Sherwood Street W1 437 2625
Savoy Hotel: Strand WC2   240 0285
Strand Palace Hotel: Strand WC2   240 3181
Tara Hotel: Wright's Lane W8   937 7211
Tower Hotel: St. Katherine's Way E1 493 1341
Westbury Hotel: Conduit Street W1 488 1276

OBTAINABLES LTD.
Panton House, 25 Haymarket SW1
839 5363/839 4416/839 4440/839 4532

PREMIER BOX OFFICE
188 Shaftesbury Avenue WC2
240 2245/240 0771/379 7622/836 4114
201 Oxford Street W1 439 4449
64 Queen Victoria Street EC4 248 2689

SEAT FINDERS
Stellars House, 47 Greencoat Place SW1 828 1678

SIDI TICKETS
161 Drury Lane WC2 242 8748

TICKET CENTRE
1b Bridge Street SW1 839 6732
23 St. Martin's Court (Charing Cross Road) WC2
240 2150

TICKETMASTER 379 6433

Alternative Cabaret

ALBANY EMPIRE
(see Section II pp. 27-28)

BATTERSEA ARTS CENTRE
(see Section II pp. 44-45)

CANAL CAFE THEATRE
(see Section II pp. 52-54)

DONMAR WAREHOUSE
(see Section II pp. 59-61)

GATE THEATRE CLUB
(see Section II pp. 70-71)

KENNETH MORE THEATRE
Oakfield Road, Ilford, Essex   553 4466

MAN IN THE MOON
(see Section II pp. 88)

MITRE
Tunnel Avenue SE10 858 0985

NORTH STAR
104 Finchley Road NW3   624 5648

PALACE BAR
Palace Theatre, Shaftesbury Avenue W1
437 4414

THREE HORSESHOES PUB
(see PENTAMETERS THEATRE,
Section II pp. 105-106)

TRAMSHED
51 Woolwich New Road SE18   855 3371

XENON
196 Piccadilly W1   734 9344

Children's Theatre

BATTERSEA ARTS CENTRE
Town Hall Road, Lavender Hill SW11 223 8413/223 6557
ages 5-12

CROYDON WAREHOUSE
62 Dingwall Road, Croydon, Surrey   680 4060
all ages

LITTLE ANGEL MARIONETTE THEATRE
14 Dagmar Passage, Cross Street N1 2DN   226 1787
all ages

MAN IN THE MOON
392 Kings Road SW3 5UZ   351 2876
ages 5-14 (drama workshops and shows)

OVAL HOUSE
54 Kennington Oval SE11   582 7680
all ages

POLKA CHILDREN'S THEATRE
240 The Broadway, Wimbledon SW19 543 4888/543 0363
all ages

TABARD THEATRE
2 Bath Road, Turnham Green W4 994 1237

TRICYCLE THEATRE
269 Kilburn High Road NW6 7JR 328 8626
4-16 (dance/drama workshops and shows)

UNICORN THEATRE
Arts Theatre, 6-7 Great Newport Street WC2H 7JB
379 3280
ages 4-12 (drama workshops and shows)

UPSTREAM THEATRE
St. Andrews, Short Street SE1 8LJ
928 5394 (BO)/633 9819 (Admin)
all ages

Concert Halls

BARBICAN CONCERT HALL
Barbican, Silk Street EC2Y 8DS
638 8891/628 8795 (BO)/638 4141(Inq.)

CENTRAL HALL, WESTMINISTER
1 Central Buildings, Westminister SW1H 9NU
222 8010 ext. 206 (BO)

CROYDON FAIRFIELD HALL
Park Lane, Croydon, Surrey
688 9291 (BO)/681 0821 (MGT)

LEWISHAM THEATRE
Catford SE6   690 3431 (BO)/690 1400 (MGT)

NEW GALLERY
123 Regent Street W1R 8HN   734 8888

PURCEL ROOM
South Bank Complex, Belvedere Road SE1 8XX
928 3191 (BO)/928 3641 (MGT)

QUEEN ELIZABETH HALL
South Bank Complex, Belvedere Road SE1 8XX
928 3191 (BO)/928 3641 (MGT)

ROYAL ALBERT HALL
Kensington Gore, Kensington Road SW7 2AP
589 8212 (BO)/589 3203 (MGT)

ROYAL FESTIVAL HALL
South Bank Complex, Belvedere Road SE1 8XX
928 3191 (BO)/928 3641

ST. JOHN'S
Smith Square, Westminister SW1
222 1061 (BO)/222 2168 (MGT)

WEMBLEY GRAND HALL
Wembley Conference Centre, Stadium Way, Wembley
HA9 0DW   902 1234 (BO)/902 8833 (MGT)

WIGMORE HALL
36 Wigmore Street W1H 9DF
935 2141 (BO)/486 1907 (MGT)

Student Theatres

CHANTICLEER THEATRE
30 Clareville Street SW7 5AP   370 4154
Theatre of the Webber Douglas
Academy—student performances.

COCKPIT
Gateforth Street NW8 8EH   402 5081 (BO)/262 7907 (MGT)
Community workshop theatre—performances by
students aged 15-23.

GOLDEN LANE THEATRE
Golden Lane EC1   638 0640
Community workshop theatre—student performances.

MACOWAN THEATRE
Logan Place W8 6QN   373 9883 (BO)/373 6932 (MGT)
Theatre of the London Academy of Music and Dramatic
Art—student performances.

MORLEY COLLEGE
61 Westminister Bridge Road SE1 7HT   928 8501
Theatre of Morley College adult education centre,
originally associated with the Old Vic—mixed student-
professional performances.

ST. GEORGE'S THEATRE
49 Tufnell Park Road, Islington N7
607 1128 (BO)/607 2288 (MGT)
Workshop in traditional Shakespearian/Elizabethan
production—student and professional performances.

SHAW THEATRE
100 Euston Road NW1 2AJ   388 7727 (BO)/388 0031 (MGT)
Home of the National Youth Theatre—student and
professional performances.

VANBRUGH THEATRE
Malet Street WC1   580 7982 (BO)/636 7076
Theatre of the Royal Academy of Dramatic Art—student
performances.

SECTION II
LONDON THEATRES A~Z

II LONDON THEATRES A-Z

Detailed information about the individual theatres is given in the following manner:

1 Theatre name: the theatres are listed in strictly alphabetical order, with cross-references where confusion might arise (e.g. Drury Lane is listed as THEATRE ROYAL DRURY LANE, but if you look under DRURY LANE you'll be directed to the right page).

2 Address and telephone numbers: map references are given for each theatre. SF refers to *Nicholson's Streetfinder*, and A-Z to Geographia's *London A-Z*.

3 A paragraph of hard information about the theatre under discussion: type of theatre (type of shows normally produced)/type of auditorium/type of stage/capacity/rating of view/rating of audibility/rating of air-conditioning/rating of heating/disabled facilities provided/number of restaurants, including booking details etc, where relevant/number of buffet, snack and other eating facilities/number of bars/other amenities/performance times of normal evening and matinée performances.

4 A brief history of the theatre, with comments on its architecture and current production policy.

5 Booking procedures: least expensive/most expensive seats/concessions: lists of people who qualify for reduced-price tickets/telephone booking: time within which each telephone booking must be paid/postal booking: cheque addressee, how to collect tickets/which credit cards accepted.

6 Getting there: *Buses* list of bus numbers which go to stops nearest the theatre, with walking directions from the stop to the theatre. *Underground* List of lines to stations nearest the theatre, again with walking directions. *British Rail* Train station nearest to the theatre, with directions as above.

Notes

All information contained in individual entries was correct at time of going to press. Note, however, that details regarding booking, prices, concessions, performance times and so on can change when a new production comes into a theatre, so it is always wise to double-check if you are uncertain.

Ratings of view, audibility, air-conditioning and heat: *** good, **fair, *poor. In regard to view, a two-star rating normally means that some seats in some sections of a theatre have restricted views (as noted), not that all or most seats provide only fair viewing. In regard to air-conditioning: a two-star or one-star rating indicates some form of effective ventilation but not fully-fledged air-conditioning. 'a-c: none' indictes no effective ventilation system whatever.

Wheelchair access to theatres is strictly regulated by London fire-safety laws. Some theatres have been granted licenses which permit seating in wheelchairs, others require wheelchairs to be folded and their occupants moved into regular seating. No theatre may admit more wheelchair spectators than its license stipulates. Therefore, it is always wise to check on the availability of wheelchair accommodation well in advance of a given performance. The note 'disabled facilities: none' in an individual entry means that the theatre has not been issued a license to admit wheelchair occupants at all.

The credit cards listed under *Booking* in each entry are those accepted by the theatre box office when you either pay for tickets in person, include your credit card number in a postal booking, or telephone book by credit card directly through the box office. The credit card booking services whose telephone numbers appear at the beginning of each entry normally accept all major credit cards. Those appearing most frequently are the Keith Prowse Agency (741 9999), Ticketmaster (379 6433), Group Sales Box Office (930 6123), and May Box Group (379 6565). In nearly all cases, no commission will be charged if you book through these services. But there are a few exceptions, so ask if a commission is being added on when you book.

As a general rule, any mainstream theatre will allow you to pay for postal bookings by including your credit card name and number plus your full mailing address and telephone number. Fringe theatres, as a general rule, prefer payment by cheque or money order when you book by post. If you are uncertain, telephone the box office.

ADELPHI THEATRE

Strand, WC2E 7NA
Map refs: SF 140 K10, A-Z 60 E4
Box Office: 836 7611, 240 7913, 240 7914 (10am-8pm
Mon-Sat)
Credit card booking: 741 9999, 836 7359, 379 6433,
240 7200 (24 hrs, 7 days per week)
Group booking: 930 6123
Stage Door: 836 9578

Mainstream (musicals, plays, reviews) / traditional audi-
torium/proscenium stage/capacity 1500/view ***/audi-
bility ***/a-c**/heat**/wheelchair seating space, disabled
rest-rooms (notify management in advance)/one coffee-
sandwich buffet/six bars/performances: 7.30pm Mon-Fri,
2.30pm Wed, 4.30 and 8pm Sat—but times can vary.

Opened as the Sans Pareil Theatre in 1806 by a soap tycoon
named Scott who wanted to show off the acting talents of
his daughter, the Adelphi was for many decades the
popular home of theatrical melodramas in London. (A real
melodrama took place there in 1897 when the much-loved
tragedian William Terriss was stabbed to death by a
madman—another actor—outside the stage door.) The
fourth and present building on the site opened in 1930 and
despite its rather sober, Modernist façade, it has housed
many of the most colourful and flamboyant musicals and
revues of the last 50 years.

BOOKING

£7-£16.50/concessions: variable with production—contact
Box Office/telephone bookings: pay within three days of
making reservation/postal booking: cheques to 'Adelphi
Theatre', include SAE/credit cards: Visa-Barclaycard,
Access-Mastercard, Diners' Club, American Express.

GETTING THERE

buses 1, 6, 9, 11, 13, 15, 23, 77, 77A, 170, 172, 176, to
Strand; theatre within a few yards. 3, 12, 24, 29, 53, 88, 159
to Trafalgar Square; walk approx. 500 yards along Strand,
theatre on left. 4, 5, 171, 188, 501, 502, 513 to Aldwych;
walk along Strand towards Trafalgar Square, then theatre
approx. 500 yards on right.

underground *Bakerloo, Jubilee or Northern Line* to Charing
Cross Station; take Strand exit, turn right into Strand and
walk approx. 500 yards towards Trafalgar Square, theatre
on right. *Piccadilly Line (Aldwych branch)* to Aldwych; take
Strand exit and walk approx. 500 yards towards Trafalgar
Square, theatre on right. *District or Circle Line* to
Embankment; take Villiers Street exit, walk away from
river up Villiers Street to Strand, turn right and walk
approx. 500 yards, theatre on right.

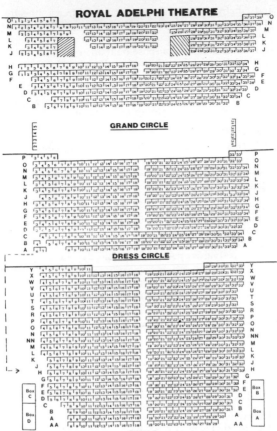

ROYAL ADELPHI THEATRE

GRAND CIRCLE

DRESS CIRCLE

STALLS

British Rail Trains to Charing Cross Station; then as from underground.

ALBANY EMPIRE

Douglas Way, Deptford, SE8
Map refs: SF 75 Z19, A-Z 80 2B
Box Office: 691 3333 (10am-8pm Tues-Sat)
Credit card booking: 691 3333

Fringe (plays, musicals)/club seating/open acting area/ capacity 300/view***/a-c**/heat**/wheelchair access/disabled rest-rooms/one buffet with bar/extras: dance, music

and dramatic workshops, and children's theatre/
performances: 8pm Tues-Sat + occasional Sunday
performances.

Opened in 1981 as a purpose-built arts centre for south-
east London, the Empire offers both a main theatre and a
small studio for workshop productions. The resident
Combination Company presents both traditional and
avante-garde works on a regular basis, with occasional
appearances by visiting touring companies.

BOOKING

£1.00-£5.50/concessions: contact Box Office/telephone
booking: collect one hour before performance/postal
booking: none/credit cards: Access-Mastercard only.

GETTING THERE

buses 1, 47, 70, 108B, 188, 288 to Evelyn Street or
Deptford High Street; walk approx 500 yards down
Deptford High Street, then right into Douglas Way. 21, 36,
36A, 36B, 53, 141, 171, 177, 184 to New Cross; walk
approx. 300 yards up Amersham Vale, then turn right into
Douglas Way.

underground *District or Metropolitan Line (East London
Section from Whitechapel Station)*; directions as for New
Cross buses.

British Rail Trains to New Cross Station; directions as
for New Cross buses.

ALBERY THEATRE

St Martin's Lane, WC2N 4AH
Map refs: SF 140 J9, A-Z 60d E3
Box Office: 836 3878 (10am-8pm Mon-Sat)
Credit card booking: 379 6565, 379 6433
Group booking: 836 3962
Stage Door: 836 5650

Mainstream (plays)/traditional auditorium/proscenium
stage/capacity 900/view ***(but front of house and boxes
a bit tricky)/audibility***/a-c**/heat**/hearing loops/no
wheelchair access/snacks/four bars/performances: 7.15pm
Mon-Fri, 2pm and 7.30pm Sat.

One of the West End's most distinguished theatres, the
Albery opened in 1903 as the New Theatre under the
management of Sir Charles Wyndham; it was renamed in
1973 in honour of Wyndham's stepson, Sir Bronson Albery,
grandfather of the present manager, Ian Albery. Behind a
handsome, neo-classical façade by W.G.R. Sprague lies a
near-perfect example of Louis XVI theatre décor, virtually
unaltered since Edwardian days. Renowned for the

Albery Theatre

consistently high quality of its productions—as are all the theatres associated with the Wyndham-Albery managerial dynasty—the Albery was home for both the Old Vic and Sadler's Wells companies during World War II, and is still remembered for its brilliant Shakespeare seasons featuring Olivier, Richardson and Gielgud.

BOOKING

£4.90-£12.50/concessions: OAPs, students, unemployed, under-24 British Rail cardholders, youth groups, some disabled (all standby tickets only), plus groups of twelve of more/telephone booking: pay within three days of making reservation/postal booking: cheques to 'Albery Theatre', with SAE/credit cards: Visa-Barclaycard, Access-Mastercard, Diners' Club, American Express.

GETTING THERE

buses 1, 24, 29, 176 to Leicester Square; walk east in Cranbourn Street, right into St Martin's Lane, theatre on right a few yards along. 3, 6, 9, 11, 12, 13, 15, 53, 77, 77A, 88, 159, 170, 172 to Trafalgar Square; walk uphill through St Martin's Place, bear right into St Martin's Lane, theatre approx. 100 yards on left. 14, 19, 22, 38, 55 to Cambridge Circus; walk downhill along Charing Cross Road for approx. 300 yards, turn left into Cranbourn Street and continue as for Leicester Square buses.

underground *Northern or Piccadilly Line* to Leicester Square; from any exit go to Cranbourn Street and continue as for Leicester Square buses. *Bakerloo or Jubilee Line* to Charing Cross Station; take Strand exit to Trafalgar Square, then proceed as for Trafalgar Square buses. *Central Line* to Tottenham Court Road; walk downhill along Charing Cross Road for approx 500 yards, turn left into Cranbourn Street, right into St Martin's Lane, theatre a few yards on right.

British Rail   Trains to Charing Cross Station; proceed from there as from Charing Cross underground.

The ALBERY

ALDWYCH THEATRE

Aldwych WC2B 4DF
Map refs: SF 141 N8, A-Z 60d F3
Box Office: 836 6404/836 0641 (10am-8pm Mon-Sat)
Credit card booking: 379 6233, 741 9999, 379 6565
Group booking: 930 6123
Stage door: 836 5537

Mainstream (plays)/traditional auditorium/proscenium stage/capacity 1092/view **/audibility ***/a-c ***/heat ***/ wheelchair access to boxes only (notify management in advance)/snacks and coffee bar/three bars/performances: 7.30pm Mon-Fri, 5pm-8.30pm Sat.

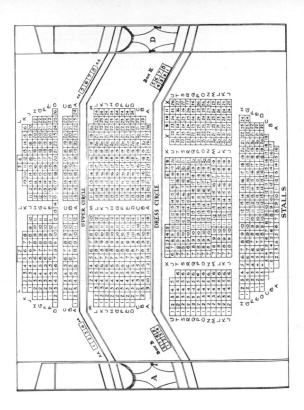

Opened in 1905, the Aldwych was designed as a companion building to the Strand Theatre a few yards away in what was then a slum redevelopment site at the bottom of Kingsway. The Aldwych's neo-classical façade, designed by W.G.R. Sprague, remains a fine example of turn-of-the-Century theatre buildings in London, but the once imposing neo-Georgian interior has suffered some ill-advised refurbishing over the years, and viewing from certain sections is rather poor. Farces—notably by Ben Travers—were the theatre's mainstay during the 1920s and 30s. More serious drama took over after World War II, and from 1960 to 1982 the Royal Shakespeare Company used the Aldwych as its London home

BOOKING

£3.00-£12.00/concessions: OAPs, students, unemployed/ telephone booking: pay within 3 working days of making reservation/postal booking: cheques to 'Aldwych Theatre', include SAE/credit cards: Visa-Barclaycard, Access-Mastercard, Diners' Club, American Express.

GETTING THERE

buses   1, 4, 5, 6, 9, 11, 13, 15, 23, 68, 77, 77A, 170, 171, 172, 176, 188, 501, 502, 513, to Aldwych Theatre beside Waldorf Hotel a few steps from Drury Lane.

underground   *Piccadilly Line* to Aldwych; directions as for Aldwych buses.

British Rail   Charing Cross Station; take Strand exit, go right along Strand approx. 500 yards, bear left into Aldwych, theatre on left just past the Waldorf Hotel.

ALMEIDA THEATRE

Almeida Street N1 1TA
Map refs: SF 133 W3, A-Z 46 3B
Box Office: 359 4404 (10am-6pm)
Credit card booking 359 4404

Fringe (plays, concerts, recitals, revue)/open auditorium/open acting area/capacity 175/view *** (check about pillars when booking)/audibility ***/a-c: none/heat **/disabled facilities: artsline 388 2227/one buffet/restaurant with bar/performances: 7pm-8pm Mon-Sat (time depends upon programme)/occasional matinées.

Founded in 1978 by the dynamic Pierre Audi in a renovated, 19th-century scientific institute the Almeida has become one of London's most exciting small theatres; staging new works by both English and foreign writers, and mounting each summer the Almeida International Festival featuring contemporary music from all over the world.

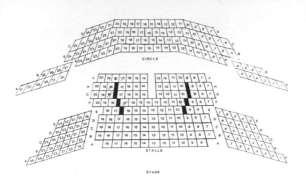

CIRCLE

STALLS

STAGE

BOOKING

£4.00-£5.00/concessions: contact box office/telephone booking: collect 1 hour before performance/postal booking: contact box office for details/credit cards: Visa-Barclaycard, Access-Mastercard.

GETTING THERE

buses 4, 19, 30, 43, 171, 277, 279 to Upper Street (ask for St. Mary's Church or nearest stop to Almeida Street); theatre on left a few steps from intersection of Upper Street and Almeida Street.

underground *Northern Line* to Angel; walk north through Angel multiple intersection to Upper Street, continue, remembering to bear left at Essex Road junction, to Almeida Street, theatre on left near corner (7-10 minute walk). *Waterloo or City Line* to Essex Road, turn right from station, down Essex Road, right in Cross Street to Upper Street, Almeida Street is opposite a few yards to left, theatre on left at corner. *Victoria Line* to Highbury and Islington; take Upper Street exit, walk down Upper Street for approx. half a mile, right in Almeida Street, theatre on left near corner.

AMBASSADORS THEATRE

West Street WC2H 9ND
Map refs: SE 140 8H, A-Z 60d D3
Box Office: 836 6111 (10am-8pm Mon-Sat)
Credit card booking: 836 1171
Stage Door: 836 4105

Mainstream (plays)/traditional auditorium/proscenium stage/capacity 460/view ***/audibility ***/a-c **/heat ***/ wheelchair access (notify management in advance)/ snacks/three bars/performance times vary with production: see press.

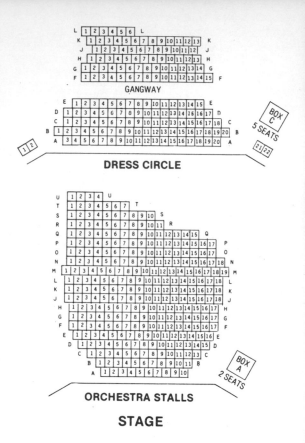

GANGWAY

BOX C
5 SEATS

DRESS CIRCLE

BOX A
2 SEATS

ORCHESTRA STALLS

STAGE

Opened in 1913, this small, inviting theatre with its handsome Louis XVI decor, was for many years the home of popular and intimate revue in London. Both Vivian Leigh and Paul Robeson made their West End débuts here, but the theatre is probably best remembered as the first home of one of history's longest-running plays, *The Mousetrap*, which ran for 8862 performances between 1952 and 1974 before transferring to the St. Martin's Theatre next door.

BOOKING

Contact box office for all details/telephone booking: pay within three days of making reservation/postal booking: cheques to 'Ambassadors Theatre', include SAE/credit cards: Visa-Barclaycard, Access-Mastercard, Diners' Club, American Express.

GETTING THERE

buses 1, 14, 19, 22, 24, 29, 38, 55, 176 to Cambridge Circus; from east side of Cambridge Circus, walk a few steps into Tower Street, then immediate right into West Street, left around corner, theatre on left a few yards along. 7, 8, 25, 73, 134 to Tottenham Court Road Station; walk down east side of Charing Cross Road to Cambridge Circus and continue as for Cambridge Circus buses. 3, 6, 11, 12, 13, 15, 23, 53, 77, 77A, 88, 159, 170, 172 to Trafalgar Square; walk uphill through St. Martin's Place (keeping National Gallery, National Portrait Gallery on left), continue straight on up east side of Charing Cross Road to Cambridge Circus, continue as for Cambridge Circus buses.

underground *Northern or Piccadilly Line* to Leicester Square; take Charing Cross Road east exit, uphill to Cambridge Circus, continue as for Cambridge Circus buses. *Central or Northern Line* to Tottenham Court Road; walk down east side of Charing Cross Road to Cambridge Circus, continue as for Cambridge Circus buses. *Bakerloo Line* to Piccadilly Circus; take Shaftesbury Avenue exit, walk up Shaftesbury Avenue to Cambridge Circus, cross to east side and continue as for Cambridge Circus buses. *Jubilee Line* to Charing Cross Station; take Strand exit to Trafalgar Square and continue as for Trafalgar Square buses.

British Rail Trains to Charing Cross Station, directions as for Charing Cross underground.

APOLLO THEATRE

Shaftesbury Avenue W1V 7HD
Map refs: SF 140 F9, A-Z 60d D3
Box Office: 437 2663, 437 2664 (10am-8pm Mon-Sat)
Credit card booking: 434 3598, 434 3599
Stage Door: 437 3435

Mainstream (plays)/traditional auditorium/proscenium stage/capacity 769/view ** (some restricted seats in dress circle/audibility ***/a-c */heat ***/two bars/performance times vary with production: see press.

With its art nouveau-flavoured Renaissance façade, imposing iron-and-glass canopy, and fine Louis XIV interior, the Apollo, which opened in 1901, is the architectural showpiece of a group of four Victorian-Edwardian theatres dominating the north side of Shaftesbury Avenue between Wardour and Great Windmill Streets.

The theatre has had a consistently successful history playing comedies, musicals and some serious drama; its most notable long-runs in recent years being Alan

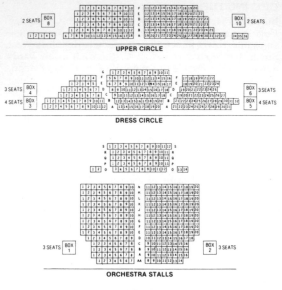

UPPER CIRCLE

DRESS CIRCLE

ORCHESTRA STALLS

STAGE

Bennet's *Forty Years On* with John Gielgud, *Home* with Gielgud and Ralph Richardson and *Boeing-Boeing* which began a 3½-year run in 1962.

BOOKING

Postal booking: cheques to 'Apollo Theatre', include SAE/ credit cards: Visa-Barclaycard, Access-Mastercard, American Express.

GETTING THERE

buses 1, 14, 19, 22, 24, 29, 38, 55, 176 to Cambridge Circus (or nearest stop in Shaftesbury Avenue to Wardour Street) from all stops, look for theatre in the group of 4 theatres on the north side of Shaftesbury Avenue approx. half-way between Cambridge Circus and Piccadilly Circus. 3, 6, 9, 12, 13, 15, 23, 53, 88, 159, to Piccadilly Circus; to Shaftesbury Avenue and continue as for Cambridge Circus buses.

underground *Bakerloo or Piccadilly Line*, Piccadilly Circus; take Shaftesbury Avenue exit and continue as for Cambridge Circus buses. *Northern Line* to Leicester Square; Cranbourn Street to Leicester Square, walk through the Square, right in Wardour Street to Shaftesbury Avenue, continue as for Cambridge Circus buses.

APOLLO VICTORIA

17 Wilton Road SW1V 1LL
Map refs: SF 147 Z4, A-Z 62c B3
Box Office: 630 6262, 828 8665 (10am-8pm Mon-Sat)
Credit card booking: 630 6262
Group booking: 828 6188
Stage Door: 834 7231

Mainstream (musicals) / traditional auditorium / proscenium stage/capacity 2500 (presently reduced to 1500 to accommodate production of *Starlight Express*)/view** (restrictions, again resulting from *Starlight Express* production, explained at time of booking)/audibility ***/a-c */heat ***/wheelchair access (notify management in advance)/three bars/confectionary stand/performances. 7.45pm Mon-Sat, 3pm Tues-Sat

Opened in 1930 as a 'super-cinema', the huge Apollo Victoria, with its striking Modernist exterior and eminently comfortable auditorium, is one of the few examples of architecturally successful 1930s theatre-building in London. Since going over to stage entertainments in the 1970s, the theatre has largely been used for major musical productions and is presently the home of Andrew Lloyd Webber's *Starlight Express*, which looks set to run for several more years.

BOOKING

£7.00-£17.50/concessions: OAPs, students, unemployed/ telephone booking: pay within 4 working days of making

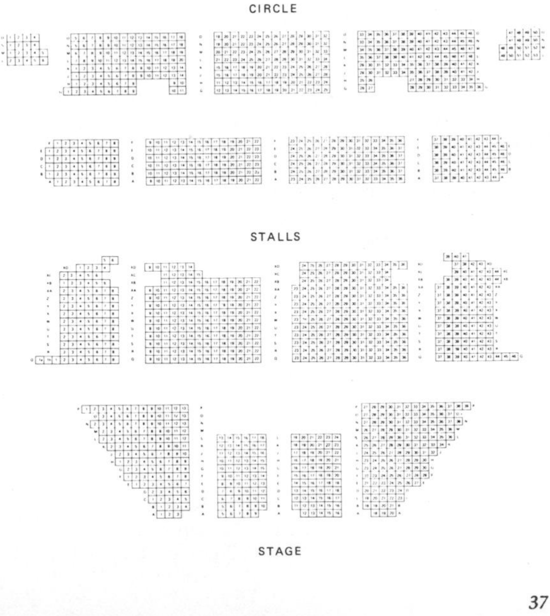

CIRCLE

STALLS

STAGE

reservation/postal booking: cheques to 'Apollo Victoria Theatre', include SAE/credit cards: Visa-Barclaycard, Access-Mastercard, Diners' Club, American Express.

GETTING THERE

buses   2, 2B, 10, 11, 16, 24, 25, 29, 36, 36A, 36B, 38, 39, 52, 52A, 55, 70, 76, 149, 185, 500, 507 to Victoria Station; from station plaza (where most buses stop), Wilton Road is the first street on the left as you face station's main entrance, theatre a few yards along on left. Also a theatre entry in Vauxhall Bridge Road.

underground   *District and Circle Line or Victoria Line* to Victoria, take station plaza exit and proceed as for Victoria buses.

British Rail   Trains to Victoria Station; station plaza exit and proceed as for Victoria buses.

ARTS THEATRE

6-7 Great Newport Street WC2H 7JB
Map refs: SF 140 H8, A-Z 60d 3E
Box Office: 836 3334/836 2132 (10am-6pm Mon-Sat)
Stage Door: 836 7545

Fringe (plays, children's theatre)/traditional auditorium/ proscenium stage/capacity 340/view ***/audibility ***/a-c: none/heat **/disabled rest rooms, hearing loops (notify management in advance)/vegetarian restaurant (10am-10.30pm)/one bar/performances: 7.00pm-8.00pm Tues-Sat/evenings, Tues-Fri 2pm, Sat & Sun 2.30pm children's shows.

Long renowned for its staging of new, experimental plays, (Beckett's *Waiting For Godot* had its London première here), the Arts, which opened as a theatre club in 1927, also came to be known as 'The Pocket National' for its fine productions of Shakespeare and other classics during Alan Clunes's term of management in the 1940s and 50s. Today, the theatre remains one of the mainstays of the London fringe.

BOOKING

£5.00 or less/contact box office for concessions/telephone booking: collect within three working days before performance/postal booking: cheques to 'Arts Theatre' (include cheque card number), include SAE/credit cards: none.

GETTING THERE

buses   1, 24, 29, 176 to Leicester Square; walk 1 block uphill in Charing Cross Road, right into Great Newport Street, theatre beside Leicester Square underground exit.

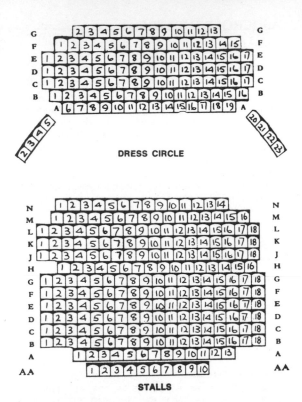

DRESS CIRCLE

STALLS

3, 6, 9, 11, 12, 13, 15, 23, 53, 77, 77A, 88, 159, 170, 172, 176 to Trafalgar Square; walk uphill through St. Martin's Place (keeping National Gallery, National Portrait Gallery on left), bear half right into Charing Cross Road, continue approx. 300 yards, right into Great Newport Street, theatre on left beside Leicester Square underground exit. 1, 14, 19, 22, 38, 55 to Cambridge Circus; walk downhill in Charing Cross Road approx. 200 yards, left into Great Newport Street, theatre on left beside Leicester Square underground exit.

underground *Piccadilly or Northern Line* to Leicester Square; Great Newport Street exit, theatre next door. *Bakerloo or Jubilee Line* to Charing Cross Station; take Strand exit to Trafalgar Square and continue as for Trafalgar Square buses. *Central Line* to Tottenham Court Road; take Charing Cross Road exit, walk downhill in Charing Cross Road to Cambridge Circus and proceed as for Cambridge Circus buses.

British Rail Trains to Charing Cross Station, proceed as for Charing Cross underground.

ASHCROFT THEATRE

Fairfield Halls, Park Lane, Croydon CR9 1DG
Map refs: SF 157 05, A-Z 118 2C
Box Office: 688 9291 (10am-8pm Mon-Sat)
Credit card booking: 680 5955 (10am-7.30pm Mon-Sat)

Mainstream (plays, musicals)/open plan auditorium with balcony/proscenium stage/capacity 763/view ***/audibility ***/a-c***/heat***/disabled seating, hearing loops, disabled rest rooms, ramps and lifts for wheelchairs/one restaurant (noon-2.30pm Mon-Sat; 6pm-8.30pm Wed, Fri + Sat, tel. 681 7181 for reservations)/one coffee shop/three bars/performances: 7.45pm Mon-Fri, 3pm + 7.45pm Sat.

Named for the distinguished British actress, Dame Peggy Ashcroft, the Ashcroft Theatre opened in 1962 as part of the newly built Croydon Civic Centre Complex. Productions since then have largely been limited to popular mainstream fare. The theatre is unusual in that its stage can be adapted automatically for either proscenium or arena presentations.

BOOKING

£4.00-£7.00/concessions: OAP, children, unemployed, students (standby only except Thurs)/telephone booking: collect-pay 48 hours before performance/postal booking: cheques to 'Fairfield Halls', include sae/credit cards: Visa-Barclaycard, Access-Mastercard, American Express, Diners' Club.

GETTING THERE

buses 12A, 50, 54, 60, 64, 68, 75, 109, 119, 119B, 130, 130B, 154, 157, 166, 166A, 190, 194, 194B, 197, 213, 289 to East Croydon Station; walk west along George Street approx. 400 yards, left into Park Lane, Fairfield Halls on left approx. 400 yards along. For buses that do not go to East Croydon Station: get off at main intersection of London Road, North End Road, Station Road, walk down North End Road approx. 500 yards, left into George Street, right into Park Lane, Fairfield Halls on left approx. 400 yards along.

British Rail Trains to East Croydon Station, turn right out of station along George Street and continue as for East Croydon Station buses (1st directions above).

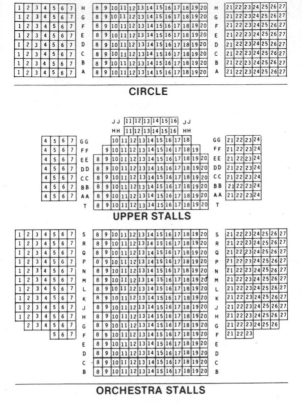

CIRCLE

UPPER STALLS

ORCHESTRA STALLS

STAGE

ASTORIA THEATRE

Charing Cross Road WC2H 0EN
Map refs: SF 140 F4-5, A-Z 60d D2
Box Office: 437 8772, 734 4287 (10am-8pm Mon-Sun)
Credit card booking: 437 8772, 734 4287
Group booking: 437 8772, 734 4287

Mainstream (musicals)/traditional auditorium/proscenium stage/capacity 839/view ***/audibility ***/a-c **/heat **/ disabled facilities: none/one sandwich and coffee bar/ three bars/performances: 8pm Tues-Sat, 4pm Sat-Sun.

Opened as a 'super-cinema' in the late 1920s just as 'talkies' came in, the Astoria prospered through the 1930s (it seated some 2000 and featured a ballroom in the basement), fell on harder times after World War II, became a theatre in the 1970s, a supper-theatre in the early '80s, and then reverted to straight stage productions last year with the opening of the popular pop-musical *Lennon*. At time of writing the show was still playing to big audiences and looked set to go on for some time.

BOOKING

£6.50-£14.50/concessions: students, (others contact box office)/telephone booking: pay within 4 days of making reservation/postal booking: cheques to 'Astoria Theatre', include SAE/credit cards: Visa-Barclaycard, Access-Mastercard, American Express.

GETTING THERE

buses 1, 7, 8, 14, 19, 22, 24, 25, 29, 38, 55, 73, 134, 176 to Tottenham Court Road Station; theatre visible at south-west corner of Tottenham Court Road and Oxford Street.

underground *Central or Northern Line* to Tottenham Court Road; take Oxford Street south exit, look for theatre entry in Charing Cross Road at intersection with Oxford Street. *Piccadilly Line* to Leicester Square; walk uphill in Charing Cross Road to Oxford Street, theatre on left at intersection.

BARBICAN CENTRE

Barbican Centre, Silk Street, EC2Y 8DS
Map refs: SF 142 B1, A-Z 61b E1
Box Office: 638 8891, 628 8759 (10am-8pm 7 days per week)
Credit card booking: 638 8891, 629 8759 (hours as above)
Information: 628 2295, 628 9760 (24-hr)
Group booking: 930 6123
Stage Door: 628 8264

Barbican Theatre Mainstream (plays, musicals, especially Shakesperean productions)/open-plan auditorium with circles/open stage/capacity 1162/view***/audibility*** /a-c***/heat***/wheelchair access and seating/induction loops/disabled rest-rooms (notify management in advance).

The Pit (studio theatre) Fringe (plays)/gallery seating/ open acting area/capacity 150-200/view ** (some restricted viewing from side seats)/audibility ***/disabled facilities: wheelchair access and seating available on request.

both theatres One restaurant (noon-3pm and 5.45pm-last orders (30 mins after last performance)/one self-service buffet restaurant/one wine bar/seven bars/ performances: 7.30pm Mon-Sat + 2pm Thurs and Sat.

Opened in 1982, the now-permanent home of the Royal Shakespeare Company provides two very differently-designed theatres for productions of all kinds, both of them housed within the vast new Barbican Centre in the

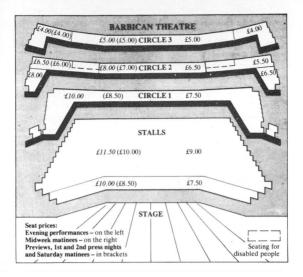

BARBICAN THEATRE

£4.00 (£4.00) £5.00 (£5.00) **CIRCLE 3** £5.00 £4.00

£6.50 (£6.00) £8.00 (£7.00) **CIRCLE 2** £6.50 £5.50

£8.00 £6.50

£10.00 (£8.50) **CIRCLE 1** £7.50

STALLS

£11.50 (£10.00) £9.00

£10.00 (£8.50) £7.50

STAGE

Seat prices:
Evening performances – on the left
Midweek matinees – on the right
Previews, 1st and 2nd press nights
and Saturday matinees – in brackets

Seating for disabled people

City of London. The RSC itself is as distinguished and as exciting an acting company as you could ever hope to see, rivalled only by the National for the quality and scope of its productions and the excellence of its acting. The architecture is more controversial. The Barbican Theatre's sweeping, open-plan stalls do house a large audience with no seat more than 65 feet from the stage, but the absence of aisles makes access difficult, and some find the seats cramped. The aptly-named Pit, somewhere in the bowels of the building, allows one to watch the RSC's most innovative work in intimate surroundings (to put it kindly); some may feel, however, that only the Pendulum is missing.

BOOKING

Barbican Theatre £5-£12.50, Pit £6.50/concessions: students, OAPs, unemployed, groups of 12+, school and college groups accompanied by lecturer/telephone booking: pay within three days of making reservation/ postal booking: cheques to 'Barbican Centre', include SAE (subscription membership available)/credit cards: Visa-Barclaycard, Access-Mastercard, Diners' Club, American Express/join mailing list for priority information and advance booking privileges.

GETTING THERE

buses 4, 8, 9, 11, 17, 21, 23, 25, 43, 76, 133, 141, 214, 271 to Barbican; ask for nearest stop to Barbican Centre and follow signs.

underground *Circle or Metropolitan Line* to Barbican; cross road to Beech Street and follow yellow line onto podium walkway, which leads to Centre. *Central, Metropolitan or Northern Line* to Moorgate; take Moorgate West exit, left out of station, left into Ropemaker Street, left again into Moor Lane, immediate right into Silk Street, then Barbican entrance a few yards along. *Central Line* to St Paul's; follow signs to Barbican.

British Rail Train to Moorgate, Barbican, Liverpool Street/Broad Street or Bank, follow signs from any station. If on entering the Centre itself you feel intimidated by the strange underwater lighting, the vast expanses of seemingly unused space, the endlessly confusing levels and the uninformative signs, you won't be the first—and if you get lost, don't despair, for you will soon be joined by others and can make up a jolly search party.

BATTERSEA ARTS CENTRE THEATRE

Town Hall, Town Hall Road, Lavender Hill SW11
Map refs: SF 88 M8, A-Z 76 C3
Box Office: 223 8413 (10am-10pm Wed-Sun, Noon-2pm Mon-Tues, Answerphone 10am-6pm Mon-Tues)
Credit card booking: 223 8413

Main theatre Fringe (plays, performance, dance)/open seating, raked, flexible/open acting area/ capacity 150/ view ***/audibility ***/a-c */heat **/wheelchair access, lift and ramps/hearing loops/rest rooms adapted for disabled (notify management in advance)/performances: 8pm Wed-Sun (times vary with production).

Studio theatre Fringe (plays, performance, experimental)/ open seating/open acting area/capacity 50/view ***/ audibility ***/a-c ***/heat **/disabled facilities: as above/ performances: 8.30pm Wed-Sun (times vary with production). Both theatres one restaurant (10am-8.30pm)/ one bar (6pm-11pm).

Centre opened in 1981, and under Anthony Fegan's artistic direction has become an important community theatre for the staging of both new works and revivals.

BOOKING

£1.50-£3.50 (plus £1.00 membership to arts centre required)/concessions: OAPs, students, under-18, unemployed (£1.00 reduction in main theatre, 50 pence reduction in Studio)/telephone bookings: pay within 3 days of making reservation/postal booking: cheques to 'Battersea Arts Centre', include SAE or collect at box office 30 minutes before performance/credit cards: Visa-Barclaycard, Access-Mastercard.

GETTING THERE

buses 45, 77, 77A to Lavender Hill, Latchmere Road

stop; walk east in Lavender Hill just a few yards to Town Hall Road, theatre on left 19, 37, 39, 49, 156, 170, 249, 295 to Clapham Junction; walk east along Lavender Hill approx. 500 yards, cross Latchmere Road, continue on another few yards to Town Hall Road, theatre on left.

underground *Northern Line* to Clapham Common; consult bus map; (approx. 1½ miles to theatre).

British Rail Trains to Clapham Junction Station, to Lavender Hill and continue as for Clapham Junction buses.

BEAR GARDEN — See Shakespeare Globe

BLOOMSBURY THEATRE

15 Gordon Street WC1H 0AH
Map refs: SF 132 F17, A-Z 45 E4
Box Office: 387 9269 (10am-8pm Mon-Sat. 6pm close if no perf.)
Credit card booking: 380 1453
Stage Door: 388 3363

Mainstream-fringe (plays, dance, mime, performance, concerts, opera)/traditional auditorium (continental design)/proscenium stage (with flexible orchestra pit lifts to create a thrust stage)/capacity 560/view *** (restricted view from slips with certain stage set arrangements—check with box office)/audibility ***/a-c **/heat **/wheelchair seating space, lifts to foyer and auditorium, adapted rest rooms/one buffet bar/one bar/performances: 7.30pm Mon-Sat/occasional 8pm start/occasional Sunday evening performances.

Opened in 1968 as a student theatre, the Bloomsbury began staging professional productions in 1974, and while still used from October to March mainly by Unversity

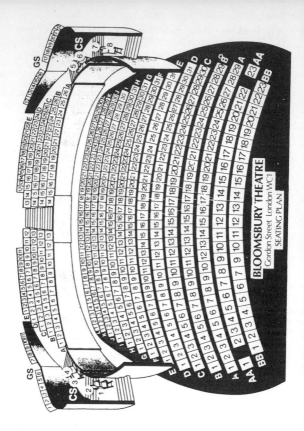

College, London, as a student venue, the theatre
continues to offer important professional productions of
new and experimental works throughout the rest of the
year.

BOOKING

£4.50-£6.50/concessions: OAPs, students, unemployed
(£2.50 per ticket), groups of 10 (1 ticket free)/telephone
booking: pay within three working days of making
reservation/postal booking: cheques to 'Bloomsbury
Theatre',include SAE/credit cards: Visa-Barclaycard,
Access-Mastercard, American Express.

GETTING THERE

buses 14, 18, 24, 27, 29, 30, 73, 134, 137, 176, 253 walk
down Gower Street (with traffic), left into Gower Place,
right into Gordon Street, theatre on right a few yards
along. (If you leave bus further down Gower Street, then

continue to Bynge Place, turn left, and left again into Gordon Street.) 14, 18, 30, 68, 73, 77A, 188 to Woburn Place at Euston Road; walk down Upper Woburn Place to Endsleigh Gardens, turn right, continue to Gordon Street, theatre just across street. (If you leave bus further down Woburn Place, walk down to Endsleigh Place, turn right, and right again into Gordon Street.)

underground *Circle or Metropolitan Line* to Euston Square; walk left into Gower Place, right into Gordon Street, theatre on right. *Northern or Victoria Line* to Euston; cross Euston road, turn left, look for Gordon Street on right, walk 1 block, theatre on right. *Northern or Victoria Line* to Warren Street; walk east along Euston Road (crossing Tottenham Court Road and Gower Street), right into Gordon Street, theatre on right 1 block along.

British Rail Trains to Euston Station; directions as for Euston Station underground.

BRIDGE LANE THEATRE

Bridge Lane, Battersea SW11
Map refs: SF 88 K3, A-Z 76 B2
Box Office: 228 8828 (answerphone), 228 5158 (10am-8pm Tues-Sat)

Fringe (plays)/arena seating/platform thrust stage/ capacity 196/view ***/audibility ***/a-c: none/heat **/wheelchair seating, hearing loops (notify management in advance)/one bar/food/patio/extras: art exhibitions, dance, music etc./performances: 7.30pm or 8pm Tues-Sat, Sun check for Box Office.

Described by *Time Out* as 'the best performance space in London', Bridge Lane specializes in staging new plays by relatively new writers along with older, neglected works of merit. Dance plays an important role at Bridge Lane productions, and the theatre's policy also includes regular seasons of work from abroad, particularly the USA.

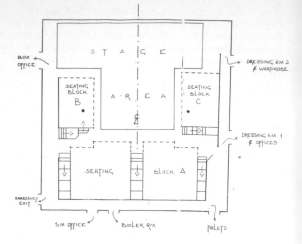

BOOKING

£2.50-£4.50/concessions: OAPs, students, unemployed, Equity members/telephone booking: collect fifteen minutes before performance/postal booking: cheques to 'Bridge Lane Theatre', SAE or collect thirty minutes before performance.

GETTING THERE

buses 19, 39, 44, 45, 49, 170 to Battersea Bridge Road at Battersea Park Road; walk a few yards up Battersea Bridge Road, bear left into Bridge Lane, theatre near corner.

BUSH THEATRE

Bush Hotel, Shepherds Bush Green, W12 8QD
Map refs: SF 136 E17, A-Z 58 C3
Box Office: 743 3388 (24 hrs)

Fringe (plays)/flexible raked seating/open acting area/ capacity 90/view ***/audibility ***/a-c ***/disabled facilities: contact box office/pub and hotel facilities/performances: 8pm Tues-Sun.

Founded in 1972 as a pub theatre in the Bush Hotel, the Bush mainly features new and experimental works by contemporary British playwrights, plus British premières of foreign plays. One of London's liveliest pub theatres, and a particularly important venue for new writing, the Bush Theatre produces six plays per year and, in addition, invites in one or two professional companies, or brings in a new play from out of town.

BOOKING

£4.50 (plus 50p membership per year)/concessions: OAPs, students, unemployed/telephone booking: collect—pay one hour before performance/postal booking: none/credit cards: none.

GETTING THERE

buses 12, 49, 72, 88, 105, 207, 220, 283, 295 to Shepherds Bush Green. Bush Hotel visible from all stops around Shepherds Bush Green.

underground *Central Line* to Shepherds Bush; cross intersection, then go right along Shepherds Bush Green until you come to the Bush Hotel. *Metropolitan Line* to Shepherds Bush; turn left along Uxbridge Road to Shepherds Bush Common, cross Common to Shepherds Bush Green, and look for Bush Hotel. *Metropolitan Line* to Goldhawk Road, turn left along Goldhawk Road until you reach 'the Green', cross the road and the theatre in on your left.

CAFÉ THEATRE UPSTAIRS

Bear and Staff Pub, 37 Charing Cross road WC2H 0DA
Map refs: SF 140 H9, A-Z 60d D3
Booking: 240 0794 (11am-11pm)

Fringe (plays)/flexible raked seating/open acting area/ capacity 40/view ***/audibility ***/a-c **/heat **/disabled facilities: none/full pub facilities downstairs, with hot meals/performances: four shows nightly—6pm, 7pm, 8pm, 9pm Mon-Sun/occasional lunchtime shows 1.30pm/ occasional late night shows. 10pm.

The Café Theatre Upstairs was founded in 1970 as the home of the Artaud Theatre Company, a group specializing in both revivals and new works. Visiting companies play the Café when the Artaud is touring, and policy is now directed toward short dramatizations of prose works by European authors such as Sartre and Dostoevsky.

BOOKING

£2.50 maximum—the more shows you see, the less the price per show/concessions: groups/telephone booking: collect—pay tickets just before show/postal booking: none/credit cards: Visa-Barclaycard, Access-Mastercard, Diners' Club, American Express (only through Fringe Box Office at the Duke of York's Theatre, tel: 379 6002).

GETTING THERE

buses 1, 24, 29, 176 to Leicester Square; pub visible directly across Charing Cross Road from Wyndham's Theatre. 3, 6, 9, 11, 12, 13, 15, 53, 77, 77A, 88, 159, 170, 172 to Trafalgar Square; walk uphill through St. Martin's Place (keeping National Gallery, National Portrait Gallery on left), continue on into Charing Cross Road, pub on left approx. 400 yards along. 14, 19, 22, 38, 55 to Cambridge Circus; walk downhill in Charing Cross Road approx. 300 yards, pub on right opposite Wyndham's Theatre.

underground *Northern or Piccadilly Line* to Leicester Square; pub visible from all Charing Cross Road exits directly across from Wyndham's Theatre. *Bakerloo or Jubilee Line* to Charing Cross Station; Strand exit to Trafalgar Square, continue as for Trafalgar Square buses. *Central Line* to Tottenham Court Road; walk down Charing Cross Road approx. 500 yards, pub on right directly across from Wyndham's Theatre.

British Rail Trains to Charing Cross Station, directions as for Charing Cross underground.

CAMBRIDGE THEATRE

Earlham Street WC2 9HU
Map refs: SF 140 J7, A-Z 60d E3
(Scheduled to reopen Spring 1987; no details available at time of going to press.)

Opened in 1930 as a home for lavish musicals and big dramatic productions, the Cambridge, still one of London's largest theatres, featured an austere modernistic façade and a strikingly original interior described by one commentator as resembling a German

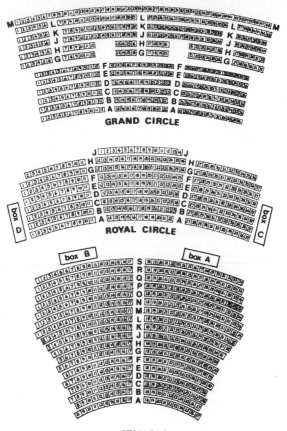

GRAND CIRCLE

ROYAL CIRCLE

box D

box C

box B

box A

STALLS

Futuristic film set. Red plush and crystal were introduced during refurbishment in the 1950s, but much of the '30s decor was retained, most notably the huge, engraved-glass bar mirrors. Beatrice Lillie was the first great star to play the Cambridge, and following a low period just before and after the Second World War, the theatre returned to its days of glory with long runs of *The Reluctant Debutante*, *Billy Liar*, *Half-a-Sixpence* starring Tommy Steele, *The Magistrate* with Alistair Sim, and in 1970 a season of National Theatre productions followed in 1972 by a much praised revival of *Journey's End*. But after the mid-70s the theatre declined again and in the early 80s had to close its doors. Recently acquired by the Stoll-Moss theatre chain, the Cambridge is presently undergoing fresh refurbishment and will reopen in the Spring of 1987.

GETTING THERE

buses 1, 14, 19, 22, 24, 38, 55, 176 to Cambridge Circus; walk east one block in Earlham Street, theatre on right at the far corner of Monmouth Street. 7, 8, 25, 73, 134 to Tottenham Court Road Station; walk down Charing Cross Road to Cambridge Circus (east side), cross Shaftesbury Avenue, left into Earlham Street continue as for Cambridge Circus buses. 3, 6, 11, 12, 13, 15, 23, 53, 77, 77A, 88, 159, 170, 172 to Trafalgar Square; walk uphill through St. Martin's Place bearing right into St. Martin's Lane, continue straight up St. Martin's Lane, Upper Street and Monmouth Street to Earlham Street, theatre on right at corner.

underground *Piccadilly Line* to Covent Garden; turn right out of station along Cranbourne, left into Neal Street, first left into Earlham, theatre one block along on left at corner of Monmouth Street. *Northern Line* to Leicester Square; Charing Cross Road (east) exit, walk uphill to Cambridge Circus and continue as for Cambridge Circus buses. *Central or Northern Line* to Tottenham Court Road and proceed as for Tottenham Court Court Road buses. *Bakerloo Line* to Piccadilly Circus; Shaftesbury Avenue exit, walk up Shaftesbury Avenue to Cambridge Circus, cross to east side and continue as for Cambridge Circus buses. *Jubilee Line* to Charing Cross Station; Strand exit to Trafalgar Square and continue as for Trafalgar Square buses.

British Rail Trains to Charing Cross Station and continue as for *Jubilee Line* underground.

CANAL CAFÉ THEATRE

Bridge House, Delamere Terrace, Little Venice W2
Map refs: SF 138 A1, A-Z 60d A1
Box Office: 289 6054 (6pm-10pm Tues-Sun, 24-hour answerphone)

Fringe (plays, reviews, satires)/club seating/platform stage/capacity 55/view ***/audibility ***/a-c (fan) **/heat *** /wheelchair access (notify management in advance)/full pub facilities including hot meals downstairs/waiter service in theatre/one bar in theatre/extra: Mon night cabaret, writers' workshop/performances: 7.45pm or 8pm, Tues-Sat, 10pm Thurs-Sun.

Opened at the Bridge House Cafe-pub in 1984 as a home for the Newsrevue Company, the Canal stages mainly small musicals and comedies, though more serious works do appear from time to time.

STAGE

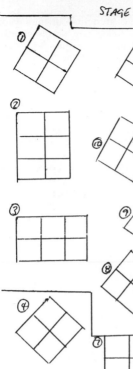

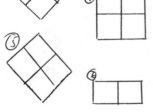

CANAL CAFE THEATRE

LITTLE VENICE
LONDON

BOOKING

£1.00-£3.50/concessions: OAPs, students, unemployed, disabled/telephone booking: collect-pay tickets shortly before performance/postal booking: cheques to 'Canal Cafe Theatre', include SAE/credit cards: none.

GETTING THERE

buses 6, 46 to Warwick Avenue Station; walk down Warwick Avenue, right into Warwick Place to Wesbourne Terrace Road, Bridge House pub on corner of Delamere Terrace. 8, 16, 16A, 176 to Edgware Road (nearest stop to Maida Avenue), or Bloomfield road to Warwick Avenue, bear right and continue along canal in Bloomfield Road, left over canal in Westbourne Terrace Road, Bridge House pub on corner of Delamere Terrace.

underground *Metropolitan Line* to Royal Oak; walk east in Harrow Road approx. 500 yards, left into Westbourne Terrace Road, Bridge House pub on corner of Delamere Terrace. *Bakerloo Line* to Warwick Avenue; directions as for Warwick Avenue bus.

British Rail Trains to Paddington Station, right from main exit, left into Bishops Bridge Road, right in Westbourne Terrace, cross Harrow Road to Wesbourne Terrace Road, Bridge House pub on corner of Delamere Terrace.

COCKPIT THEATRE

Gateforth Street NW8 8EH
Map refs: SF 130 J17, A-Z 44 B4
Box Office: 402 5081 (10am-5pm and 6pm-9pm Mon-Fri)

Fringe (plays, performance)/open seating, raked, flexible/adaptable stage: arena, thrust, platform/capacity 120-240 depending on stage arrangement/view ***/audibility ***/a-c */heat **/wheelchair access and space (notify management in advance)/one snack bar/no bar/extra: theatre-related workshops/performances: variable with company and production—contact Box Office, normally evening performances only.

Opened in 1970, the Cockpit was purpose-built by the Inner London Educational Authority (ILEA) as a training centre and public theatre dealing in a wide range of theatrical and other creative activities. New writing for the stage is emphasized, and the Cockpit features productions by both local and touring professional companies.

BOOKING

50p-£2.50/concessions: OAPs, students, under-16, unemployed, groups of five or more/telephone booking: pay within three days of making reservation/postal booking: cheques to 'Cockpit Theatre', include SAE or collect at box office/credit cards: none.

GETTING THERE

buses   6, 8, 16 16A, 176 to Edgware Road (nearest stop to Church Street); walk North-East in Church Street, crossing Penfold Street and Salisbury Street, left into Gateforth Street, theatre on left. 159 to Lisson Grove, (nearest stop to Church Street); Church Street one block, right into Gateforth Street, theatre on left.

underground   *Bakerloo Line* to Marylebone; to Lisson Grove, along Lisson Grove approx. 400 yards, left into Church Street, right into Gateforth, theatre on left. *District or Circle Line, or Metropolitan Line* to Edgware road; walk north in Edgware road to Church Street and continue as for Edgware Road buses.

British Rail   Trains to Marylebone Station, directions as for Marylebone underground.

COLISEUM—See London Coliseum

COMEDY THEATRE

Panton Street SW1Y 4DN
Map refs: SF 140 G10, A-Z 60d D4
Box Office: 930 2578 (10am-8pm Mon-Sat)
Credit card booking: 839 1438
Stage Door: 839 4474

Mainstream (plays)/traditional auditorium/proscenium stage/capacity 820/view *** (but check pillars)/audibility *** /a-c **/heat **/wheelchair seating (notify management in advance)/three bars/performance times vary with production: see press.

Designed by the renowned Victorian theatre architect Thomas Verity and opened in 1881, the Comedy displayed a classical façade and Renaissance interior which became models for later Victorian and Edwardian theatres built in London. True to the name, comedies and revues were the theatre's mainstays for several decades after its opening; but in 1956 the Watergate Theatre Club took up residence here, and protected by its 'private'

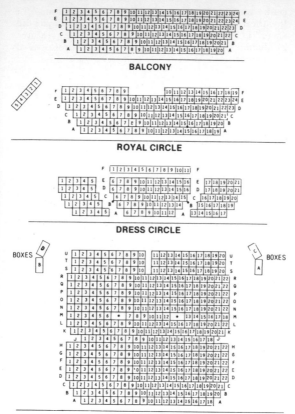

BALCONY

ROYAL CIRCLE

DRESS CIRCLE

BOXES

BOXES

ORCHESTRA STALLS

STAGE

status began staging a series of major but unlicensed dramatic works in defiance of the then still operative censorship laws. Both Arthur Miller's *A View from the Bridge* and Tennessee Williams's *Cat on a Hot Tin Roof* had their London premières at the Comedy; and since the lifting of censorship in 1968 the theatre has continued to mix programmes of serious drama, lighter comedies and occasional musicals.

BOOKING

Contact box office/telephone booking: pay within four days before performance/postal booking: cheques to 'Comedy Theatre',include SAE/credit cards: Visa-Barclaycard, Access-Mastercard, Diners' Club, American Express.

GETTING THERE

buses 3, 6, 9, 12, 13, 14, 15, 19, 22, 23, 38, 53, 55, 88, 159 to Piccadilly Circus; walk down Haymarket, left into Panton Street, theatre on right. 1, 3, 6, 9, 11, 12, 13, 15, 23, 24, 29, 53, 77, 77A, 88, 159, 170, 172, 176 to Trafalgar Square; walk down Pall Mall East, right into Haymarket right into Panton Street, theatre on right.

underground *Bakerloo or Piccadilly Line* to Piccadilly Circus; take Haymarket exit and continue as for Piccadilly Circus buses.

British Rail Trains to Charing Cross Station, from main exit walk diagonally across Trafalgar Square to Pall Mall East, then proceed as for Trafalgar Square buses.

COTTESLOE — see National Theatre

COVENT GARDEN — See Royal Opera House

CRITERION THEATRE

Piccadilly Circus W1V 9LB
Map refs: SF 140 E10, A-Z 60c C4
Box Office: 930 3216 (10am-8pm Mon-Sat)
Credit card booking: 379 6565, 379 6433, 741 9999
Group booking: 836 3962
Stage Door: 930 0991

Mainstream (plays, revues)/traditional auditorium/ proscenium stage/capacity 602/view ** (some slightly restricted areas—sold last)/audibility ***/a-c ***/heat ***/ wheelchair seating in balcony. Help is available to carry disabled to other seating sections (notify management in advance)/snacks/two bars/performance times vary with production: see press.

One of London's most intimate, attractive and comfortable West End theatres, the Criterion, designed by Thomas Verity in 1874, has the unique distinction of being located entirely under ground. The restaurant building directly above displays a handsome classical façade in the Verity style, and the auditorium—said by many to be Verity's finest work—remains virtually unaltered from the time of its slight modification in 1884. Historically, the theatre has always been known for its elegant comedies and farces, as well as its intimate revues.

BOOKING

Concessions: OAPs, students, under 24 Railcard Holders and registered deaf and blind, unemployed; groups of 12 or more (contact box office for details)/telephone booking: pay within five days of making reservation/postal booking: cheques to 'Criterion Theatre', include SAE/credit cards: Visa-Barclaycard, Access-Mastercard, Diners' Club, American Express.

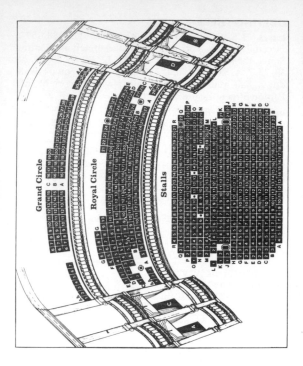

GETTING THERE

buses 3, 6, 9, 12, 13, 14, 15, 19, 22, 23, 38, 53, 55, 88, 159 to Piccadilly Circus; theatre visible at corner of Lower Regent Street and Coventry Street just off Piccadilly Circus. 1, 24, 29, 176 to Cambridge Circus; walk down Shaftesbury Avenue to Piccadilly Circus, cross to intersection of Lower Regent Street and Coventry Street, theatre on corner. 11, 77, 77A, 170, 172 to Trafalgar Square; walk down Pall Mall East, right into Lower Regent Street, continue to Coventry Street, theatre on corner.

underground *Bakerloo or Piccadilly Line* to Piccadilly Circus; Lower Regent Street exit and continue as for Piccadilly Circus buses.

British Rail Trains to Charing Cross Station, take main exit, walk diagonally across Trafalgar Square to Pall Mall East, continue as for Trafalgar Square buses.

DOMINION THEATRE

Tottenham Court Road W1P 0AG
Map refs: SF 140 G4, A-Z 60d D2
Box Office: 580 9562, 636 8538 (10am-8pm Mon-Sat)
Credit card booking: 836 2428 (24-hour 7-day-week)
Group booking: 930 6123
Information: 580 8845
Stage Door: 636 2656

Mainstream shows, (musicals)/traditional auditorium/
proscenium stage/capacity 2005/view***/audibility***/a-c*
/heat*/disabled facilities: contact box office/snacks/four
bars/performances: 7.30pm Mon-Fri, 2.30pm Thurs, 5pm
& 8.30pm Sat.

Opened in 1929 on the site of a demolished brewery, the
Dominion was briefly the home of spectacular musical
comedies in London before being transformed into a
movie palace in 1932. Now, 54 years later, the theatre has
returned to its roots, as it were, and has begun staging
musicals again.

BOOKING

£7.50-£18.50/concessions: contact box office/telephone
booking: pay within three days of making reservation/
postal booking: cheques to 'Dominion Theatre',include
SAE/credit cards: Visa-Barclaycard, Access-Mastercard.

GETTING THERE

buses 1, 7, 8, 14, 19, 22, 24, 25, 29, 38, 55, 73, 134, 176 to
Tottenham Court Road Station; theatre visible at north-
east corner of Tottenham Court Road and Oxford Street.

underground *Central or Northern Line* to Tottenham
Court Road; take Tottenham Court Road east exit, theatre
just beside station. *Piccadilly Line* to Leicester Square; walk
uphill in Charing Cross Road to Oxford Street, theatre
visible on right just across intersection.

DONMAR WAREHOUSE

41 Earlham Street WC2H 9LD
Map refs: SF 140 7J, A-Z 60d E3
Box Office: 240 8230 (Noon-7.30pm Mon-Sat)
Credit card booking: 379 6565, 379 6433
Stage Door: 240 2766

Fringe (plays)/open raked seating on 3 sides/open acting
area/capacity 244/view ***/audibility ***/a-c **/heat **/
disabled facilities: none/snacks/one bar/extras: theatre
workshops, recitals, poetry and play readings, late-night
cabaret/performances: 7.30pm or 8pm Mon-Sat, 11pm Fri-
Sat.

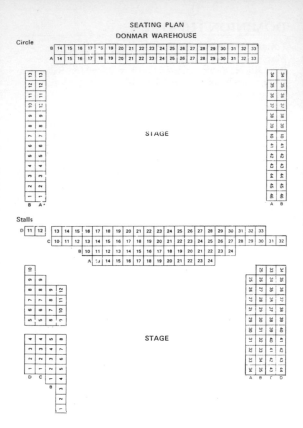

SEATING PLAN
DONMAR WAREHOUSE

'Located in the heart of the West End, the Donmar is one of London's most important small fringe venues, (from 1978 to 1982 the RSC used it as a studio for experimental works), staging new plays and classical revivals by major fringe touring companies in the . evenings, and augmenting its activities with topical late-night cabaret and revue. Managed as a non-profit charity by the admirable Ian Albery of Wyndham's theatres, the Donmar, along with larger theatres like the Royal Court and the Mermaid, serves as a splendid example of the spirit and enthusiasm that keeps English drama alive in these financially precarious times.

BOOKING

£5.90-£11.00, £4.00 late nights/concessions: contact box office/telephone booking: check procedure at time of booking/postal booking: cheques to 'Donmar Warehouse',include SAE/credit cards: Visa-Barclaycard, Access-Mastercard, Diners', Club, American Express.

GETTING THERE

buses 1, 14, 19, 22, 24, 29, 38, 55, 176 to Cambridge Circus; walk down Earlham Street approx. 300 yards, theatre on left near intersection with Neal Street. 7, 8, 25, 73, 134 to Tottenham Court Road Station (St. Giles Circus); down Charing Cross Road to Cambridge Circus, left into Earlham Street, continue as for Cambridge Circus buses. 5, 68, 77A, 172, 188, 501 to Holborn Station; walk down Kingsway approx. 200 yards, right into Great Queen Street, continue across Drury Lane into Long Acre, right into Neal Street, theatre on left across intersection with Earlham Street.

underground *Piccadilly Line* to Covent Garden; turn right out of station, left into Neal Street, theatre on left across intersection with Earlham Street. *Central or Northern Line* to Tottenham Court Road; directions as for Tottenham Court Road buses.

DRILL HALL

16 Chenies Street WC1E 7ET
Map refs: SF 132 E20, A-Z 60d D1
Box Office: 637 8270 (plus answerphone)
Credit card booking: 631 5107

Fringe (plays, performance)/raked seating (plus club seating for cabaret)/open acting area/capacity 206 (250 with tables)/view ***/audibility ***/a-c ***/heat ***/wheelchair access, ramps, disabled rest-rooms, hearing induction loop/one vegetarian restaurant/one bar/extras: under-5 child care Fri-Sat (free: book in advance), workshops/performances: 8pm Tues-Sat.

Opened in 1976, as a home for the political theatre company Action Space, the Drill Hall has now opened its doors to more diversely oriented companies. Policy still leans toward socially relevant material, however, and productions remain as exciting and well-staged as ever.

BOOKING

£3.50-£4.00/concessions £2.50: OAPs, students, unemployed, nurses, Camden residents/telephone booking: collect-pay 45 minutes before performance/postal booking: cheques to 'Drill Hall Arts Centre', include SAE.

SEATING PLAN
Front Row is optional, and is
in sections of two seats.

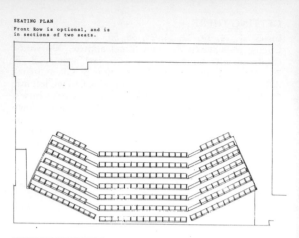

GETTING THERE

buses 14, 24, 29, 134, 176 to Chenies Street and Tottenham Court Road (or nearest stop, northbound buses), Chenies Street and Gower Street (or nearest stop, southbound buses); to Chenies Street and look for Drill Hall Arts Centre. 18, 27, 30, 73, 137 to Euston Square Station; walk down Gower Street (with traffic) or Tottenham Court Road (against traffic) approx. 1000 yards, turn into Chenies Street, look for Drill Hall Arts Centre.

underground *Circle or Metropolitan Line* to Euston Square; walk down Gower Street approx. 1000 yards, right into Chenies Street, look for Drill Hall Arts Centre. *Northern or Victoria Line* to Warren Street; walk down Tottenham Court Road approx. 1000 yards, left into Chenies Street, look for Drill Hall Arts Centre. *Northern Line* to Goodge Street; walk across Tottenham Court Road into Cheyne Street. Drill Hall on right, 400 yards approx.

British Rail Trains to Euston Road exit to Gower Street, continue as for Euston Square underground.

DRURY LANE— See Theatre Royal, Drury Lane

DUCHESS THEATRE

Catherine Street, Covent Garden WC2B 5LΛ
Map refs: SF 141 N8, A-Z 60d F3
Box Office: 836 8243 (10am-8pm Mon-Sat)
Credit card booking: 240 9648, 379 6433, 240 7200 (24-hour 7-days-week)
Stage Door: 836 3356

Mainstream (plays)/traditional auditorium/proscenium stage/capacity 487/view ***/audibility ***/a-c: **/heat **/ disabled facilities: none/one wine-coffee bar/one bar/ performance times vary with production: see press.

The little Duchess, with its neo-Tudor façade and inventively designed auditorium, is one of the most agreeable theatres imaginable in which to watch a play. Built by Ewan Barr in 1929, the Duchess, for all its minimal size, has had a most distinguished career as a home for both serious drama and 'the better sort' of comedy. T.S. Eliot's *Murder in the Cathedral* had its London début here in 1936, and numbered among its many successful long runs are Noel Coward's *Blithe Spirit* and the Emlyn Williams thriller *Night Must Fall*. In 1960 the Duchess claimed the distinction of being the first mainstream West End theatre to stage a play by Harold Pinter when *The Caretaker* transferred from the Arts Theatre Club.

BOOKING

Contact box office/pay within three days of making reservation/postal booking: cheques to 'Duchess Theatre',include SAE/credit cards: Visa-Barclaycard, Access-Mastercard, American Express.

GETTING THERE

buses 1, 4, 5, 6, 9, 11, 13, 15, 23, 68, 77, 77A, 170, 171, 172, 176, 188, 501, 502, 513 to Aldwych; from west end of Aldwych walk approx. 200 yards along Aldwych (with traffic), left into Catherine Street, theatre on left. From top

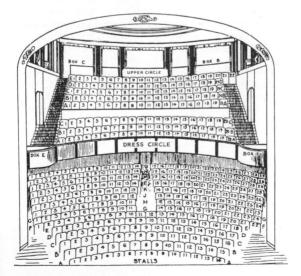

or east end of Aldwych walk along Aldwych (against traffic), right into Catherine Street, theatre on left.

underground *Piccadilly Line* to Aldwych; take Aldwych exit and continue as for Aldwych buses. *District or Circle Line* to Temple; to Strand, cross Strand, half left up Montreal Street, to Aldwych, left along Aldwych, right into Catherine Street, theatre on left. *Bakerloo, Jubilee or Northern Line* to Charing Cross Station; take Strand exit, right along Strand to Aldwych, left into Aldwych, left into Catherine Street, theatre on left. (10 minute walk)

British Rail Trains to Charing Cross Station, directions as for Charing Cross underground.

DUKE OF YORK'S THEATRE

St. Martin's Lane WC2N 4BG
Map refs: SF 140 J10, A-Z 60d E4
Box Office: 836 5122 (10am-8pm Mon-Sat)
Credit card booking: 836 9837, 741 9999
Group booking: 836 5123
Stage Door: 836 4615

Mainstream (plays)/traditional auditorium/proscenium stage/capacity 649/view ** (some restricted seats—sold last)/audibility ***/a-c **/heat ***/two wheelchair spaces in Royal circle, hearing loops, disabled rest-rooms (notify management in advance)/snacks/two bars/performances: 8pm Mon-Fri, 3pm Thurs, 5pm & 8.30pm Sat.

Opened in 1892 as the Trafalgar Square Theatre and renamed in 1895, the Duke of York's is noted architecturally for the ornamental glass and iron canopy that spans its entrance doors and for the gracefully designed neo-Renaissance interior featuring fine plasterwork and a most impressive domed ceiling. The ghost of the theatre's first manager, actress Violet Melnotte, is still thought to roam the galleries, as ill-tempered today as she was in life; but her presence has done no harm to the Duke's reputation as one of the West End's most successful theatres. *Peter Pan* had its London début here in 1904, and programmes have since featured works by Shaw, Maugham, Coward and Anouilh.

BOOKING

£5.00-£11.50/concessions: OAPs, students, unemployed (all standby on sale half an hour before performance), groups of 20 get 1 free ticket/telephone booking: pay within four days of making reservation/postal booking: cheques to 'Duke of York's Theatre', include SAE/credit cards: Visa-Barclaycard, Access-Mastercard, Diners', Club, American Express/Fringe Theatre Box Office tel. 379 6002.

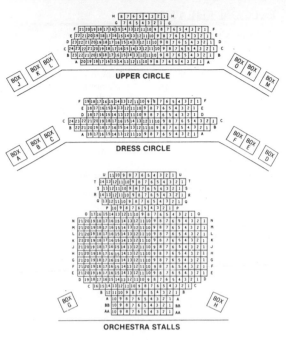

UPPER CIRCLE

DRESS CIRCLE

ORCHESTRA STALLS

STAGE

GETTING THERE

buses 1, 24, 29, 176 to Leicester Square; walk down Charing Cross Road to top of St. Martin's Place, sharp left around corner into St. Martin's Lane, theatre on left just a few yards along. (Alternatively, cut through either Cecil Court or St. Martin's Court from Charing Cross Road to St. Martin's Lane and you'll be just a few yards away). 3, 6, 9, 11, 12, 13, 15, 23, 53, 77, 77A, 88, 159, 170, 172 to Trafalgar Square; walk uphill through St. Martin's Place, bear half right into St. Martin's Lane, theatre on left just a few yards along. 14, 19, 38, 55 to Cambridge Circus; walk downhill in Charing Cross Road, left into Newport Street, right into St. Martin's Lane, theatre on right approx. 100 yards along.

underground *Piccadilly Line, Northern Line* to Leicester Square; Charing Cross Road exit, continue as for Leicester Square buses. *Bakerloo Line, Jubilee Lane* to Charing Cross Station; Strand exit to Trafalgar Square, continue as for Trafalgar Square buses.

British Rail Trains to Charing Cross Station, directions as for Charing Cross underground.

FALCON THEATRE

234 Royal College Street NW1
Map refs: SF 47 U20, A-Z 45 D2
Booking: 485 3834 (11am-8pm Mon-Sat)

Fringe (plays)/flexible raked seating/open acting area/
capacity 80/view***/audibility***/a-c none/heat*/wheel-
chair access, adapted rest-rooms/full pub facilities: hot
meals/extras: Sun jazz, other music, poetry readings/
performances: 1pm & 8pm Mon-Sat.

Founded in 1983 in a back room at the Falcon Pub with the
aid of actors John Hurt and Denholm Elliot, the Falcon
Theatre is rapidly developing a reputation for its
provocative productions of politically-oriented works
with a particularly Irish flavour.

BOOKING

£1.50 (lunchtime)-£3.50/concessions: OAPs, students, unemployed, groups of 8 or more/telephone booking:
collect-pay before performance/postal booking: none/
credit cards: none.

GETTING THERE

buses 46 to Royal College Street (nearest stop to Wilmot
Place); Falcon Pub at corner of Royal College Street and
Wilmot Place. 29, 253 to Camden Road (nearest stop to
Royal College Street); to Royal College Street, walk north
(toward Kentish Town Road), Falcon Pub at corner of
Wilmot Place. 3, 24, 27, 31, 53, 68, 74, 134, 137, 214 to
Camden Town Station; walk up Camden Road, left into
Royal College Street, Falcon Pub at corner of Wilmot
Place.

underground *Northern Line*, directions as for Camden
Town Station bus.

British Rail Trains to Camden Road Station, left into
Royal College Street, Falcon Pub a few yards along at
corner of Wilmot Place.

FINBOROUGH ARMS

Finborough Arms, Finborough Road SW10
Map refs: SF 145 Y13, A-Z 59 F4
Booking: 373 3842 (answerphone)

Fringe (plays)/flexible seating/open acting area/capacity
60/view***/audibility***/a-c none/heat**/disabled facilities:
none/pub facilities downstairs/performances: 7pm Tues-
Sun, 10pm Sat (cabaret).

A pub theatre presenting new works by its resident
company and by visiting groups. Also theatre workshop
activities.

BOOKING

£1.50-£3.00/concessions: OAPs, students, unemployed/ telephone booking: collect-pay fifteen minutes before performance/ no advance booking for Saturday cabaret/ postal booking: none/credit cards: none.

GETTING THERE

buses 30, 31, 74 to Old Brompton Road at Finborough Road (northbound buses) or at Earl's Court Road (southbound buses); from Finborough Road stop: walk down Finborough Road approx. 300 yards, Finborough Arms Pub on right at intersection of Ifield Road. From Earl's Court Road stop; walk right along Old Brompton Road 2 blocks, left into Finborough Road, continue as above.

underground Earl's Court; *District Line*, Warwick Road exit, left out of station down Warwick Road, cross Old Brompton Road, or down Finborough Road, Finborough Arms Pub on right approx. 300 yards along at intersection of Ifield Road.

FORTUNE THEATRE

Russell Street WC2B 5HA
Map refs: SF 140 M8, A-Z 60d F3
Box Office: 836 2238, 6 2239 (10am-8pm Mon-Sat)
Credit card booking: 836 2238, 741 9999

Mainstream (plays, musicals)/traditional auditorium/ proscenium stage/capacity 440/view***/audibility***/ a-c***/heat***/wheelchair seating (notify management in advance)/snacks/two bars/performances: 8pm Mon-Thurs, 8.30pm Sat, Mats Thurs + Sat 3pm.

Named after the famous Elizabethan theatre built by Philip Henslowe in 1600, the present Fortune theatre opened in 1924, had some initial success with works by Sean O'Casey in the late 1920s, and then went through a period as modest as its almost featureless exterior until 2 successive, long-running revues, 'Flanders and Swann' followed by 'Beyond the Fringe' fittingly revived its fortunes in the late 1940s and early 50s. Since then the theatre has continued to stage mainly revues, fringe transfers and musicals with consistent success.

BOOKING

£5.00-£10.50/concessions: contact box offices/telephone booking: pay within four working days of making reservation/postal booking: cheques to 'Fortune Theatre', include SAE/credit cards: Visa-Barclaycard, Access-Mastercard, Diners'Club, American Express.

GETTING THERE

buses 1, 4, 5, 6, 9, 11, 13, 15, 23, 68, 77, 77A, 170, 171, 172,

UPPER CIRCLE

BOX D

G	18	17	16	15	14	13	12	11	10	9	8	7		6	5	4	3	2	1
F	18	17	16	15	14	13	12	11	10	9	8	7		6	5	4	3	2	1
E	18	17	16	15	14	13	12	11	10	9	8	7		6	5	4	3	2	1
D	18	17	16	15	14	13	12	11	10	9	8	7		6	5	4	3	2	1
C	18	17	16	15	14	13	12	11	10	9	8	7		6	5	4	3	2	1
B	18	17	16	15	14	13	12	11	10	9	8	7		6	5	4	3	2	1
A	17	16	15	14	13	12	11	10	9	8	7	6			5	4	3	2	1

BOX C

UPPER CIRCLE

DRESS CIRCLE

BOX B

G														6	5	4	3	2	1
F	17	16	15	14	13	12	11	10	9	8	7	6		5	4	3	2	1	
E	17	16	15	14	13	12	11	10	9	8	7	6		5	4	3	2	1	
D	17	16	15	14	13	12	11	10	9	8	7	6		5	4	3	2	1	
C	17	16	15	14	13	12	11	10	9	8	7	6		5	4	3	2	1	
B	17	16	15	14	13	12	11	10	9	8	7	6		5	4	3	2	1	
A		16	15	14	13	12	11	10	9	8	7	6		5	4	3	2	1	

BOX A

DRESS CIRCLE

ORCHESTRA STALLS

L						15	14	13	12	11	10	9	8	7	6	5	4	3	2	1
K		19	18	17	16	15	14	13	12	11	10	9	8	7	6	5	4	3	2	1
J		19	18	17	16	15	14	13	12	11	10	9	8	7	6	5	4	3	2	1
H		19	18	17	16	15	14	13	12	11	10	9	8	7	6	5	4	3	2	
G		19	18	17	16	15	14	13	12	11	10	9	8	7	6	5	4	3	2	1
F	20	19	18	17	16	15	14	13	12	11	10	9	8	7	6	5	4	3	2	1
E	20	19	18	17	16	15	14	13	12	11	10	9	8	7	6	5	4	3	2	1
D		19	18	17	16	15	14	13	12	11	10	9	8	7	6	5	4	3	2	1
C			17	16	15	14	13	12	11	10	9	8	7	6	5	4	3	2	1	
B			16	15	14	13	12	11	10	9	8	7	6	5	4	3	2	1		
A				14	13	12	11	10	9	8	7	6	5	4	3	2	1			

ORCHESTRA STALLS

STAGE

176, 188, 501, 502, 513 to Aldwych; walk up Drury Lane 2 blocks, left into Russell Street, theatre on right a few yards along.

underground *Piccadilly Line* to Covent Garden; right out of station into Long Acre, right down Bow Street, left into Russell Street, theatre on left near corner of Drury Lane. *Northern Line* to Leicester Square; from any exit take Cranbourn Street to Long Acre and continue on as for Covent Garden underground.

British Rail Trains to Charing Cross Station, Strand exit, right in Strand approx. 500 yards, left up Wellington Street, right into Russell Street, theatre on left near corner of Drury Lane.

GARRICK THEATRE

Charing Cross Road WC2H 0HH
Map refs: SF 140 H10, A-Z 60d E4
Box Office: 836 4601/2 (10am-8pm Mon-Sat)
Credit card booking: 379 6433
Stage Door: 836 8271

Mainstream (plays)/traditional auditorium/proscenium
stage/capacity 656/view ***/audibility ***/a-c */heat ***/
disabled facilities: contact management in advance/two
bars/ performance times vary with production: see press.

A police station now stands on the site of the original
Garrick Theatre in Leman Street (not, one presumes, what
the theatre's famous namesake would have had in mind).
The present Garrick, built for W.S. Gilbert in 1889, opened
with a play by Pinero and has continued to the present day
to thrive largely on a mixed diet of comedy, comedy-
drama, and farce. Since 1982, the theatre was the home of
one of history's longest-running low comedies, *No Sex
Please—We're British*; presumably not what Mr. Garrick
would have had in mind, either. He would, however,
have liked the look of the theatre, with its imposing neo-

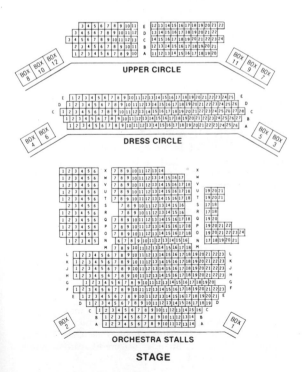

classical façade, strongly vertical auditorium design, and splendid central chandelier. The ghost of actor Arthur Bouchier, Garrick manager at the turn of the century, is said by some still to haunt the place. A notorious hater of newspaper critics, Bouchier became famous in his day for banning from the theatre the then greatly respected *Times* critic Alfred Bingham Walkley; but whether it is the termerity of subsequent generations of critics in continuing to enter his theatre that keeps Mr. Bouchier's ghost hanging about has never been ascertained.

BOOKING

Telephone booking: pay within three days of making reservation/postal booking: cheques to 'Garrick Theatre',include SAE/credit cards: Visa-Barclaycard, Access-Mastercard, American Express.

GETTING THERE

buses 1, 24, 29, 176 to Leicester Square; walk downhill in Charing Cross Road, theatre on left at top of St. Martin's Place.

underground *Bakerloo Line, Jubilee Line* to Charing Cross Station; Strand exit to Trafalgar Square, continue as for Trafalgar Square buses.

British Rail Trains to Charing Cross Station, directions as for Charing Cross underground.

GATE THEATRE CLUB

Prince Albert Pub, 11 Pembridge Road W11
Map refs: SF 137 T11, A-Z 59 F2
Box Office: 229 0706 (11am-7.30pm Mon-Sat)

Fringe (plays)/fixed raked seating/platform end stage/ capacity 65/view ***/audibility ***/a-c: none/heat: none/ disabled facilities: none/pub downstairs: no food/ performances: 7.30pm Mon-Sat/occasional Sunday performances/occastional 10pm start.

Founded in 1979 in a large banquet room above the Prince Albert Pub, the Gate Theatre Club mounts a lively mixture of new plays, adaptations, revivals of neglected older works, cabaret and late-night entertainments presented either by its own resident company or by touring groups.

BOOKING

£2.50-£4.00/concessions: OAPs, students, unemployed/ telephone booking: collect-pay tickets 30 minutes before performance/postal booking: cheques to 'Gate Theatre Company Limited', include SAE/credit cards: none/ membership required.

GETTING THERE

buses 12, 27, 28, 31, 52, 52A, 88 to Notting Hill Gate; look for Prince Albert Pub a few yards along Pembridge Road near intersection with Notting Hill Gate.

underground *Central Line, District or Circle Line* to Notting Hill Gate; directions as for Notting Hill Gate buses.

GLOBE THEATRE

Shaftesbury Avenue W1V 8AR
Map refs: SF 140 E9, A-Z 60d D3
Box Office: 437 1592 (10am-8pm Mon-Sat)
Stage Door: 437 6003

Mainstream (plays)/traditional auditorium/proscenium stage/capacity 897/view ***/audibility ***/a-c */heat ***/ wheelchair access (notify management in advance)/four bars/performance times vary with production: see press.

Built in 1906 by the eminent theatre designer W.G.R. Sprague, the Globe stands second on the right in the group of 4 theatres which dominate the north side of Shaftesbury Avenue below Cambridge Circus. Opened originally as the Hicks Theatre and meant as a companion building to the now drastically renovated Queens

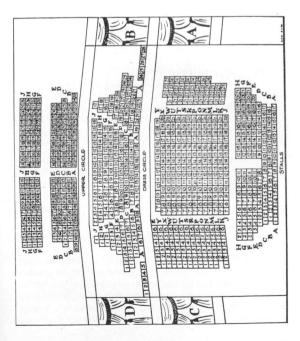

Theatre, the Globe displays a fine new-classical façade of Portland stone topped by a handsome stone cuppola, and features a splendidly ornate Louis XVI interior built to a circular plan. The theatre has been consistently successful from the year of its opening, (it was renamed in 1909 by its new manager, Charles Frohman), staging works of serious drama and top comedy in roughly equal proportion.

BOOKING

Prices vary/telephone booking: pay within three days of making reservation/postal booking: cheques to 'Globe Theatre', include SAE/credit cards: Visa-Barclaycard, Access-Mastercard, American Express.

GETTING THERE

buses 1, 14, 19, 22, 24, 38, 55, 176 to Cambridge Circus (or nearest stop in Shaftesbury Avenue to Wardour Street); from all stops, look for theatre in the group of 4 theatres on the north side of Shaftesbury Avenue approx. half way between Cambridge Circus and Piccadilly Circus. 3, 6, 9, 12, 13, 15, 23, 53, 88, 159 to Piccadilly Circus; to Shaftesbury Avenue and continue as for Cambridge Circus buses.

underground *Northern Line* to Leicester Square; Cranbourn Street to Leicester Square, walk through square, right in Wardour Street to Shaftesbury Avenue, theatre across street to the left of the Queen's Theatre.

GREENWICH THEATRE

Crooms Hill, Greenwich SE10 8ES
Map refs: SF 76 H18, A-Z 81 D2
Box Office: 858 7755 (10am-8.30pm Mon-Sat)
Credit card booking: 853 3800
Stage Door: 858 2265

Mainstream (plays, musicals)/traditional auditorium/ open thrust stage/capacity 426/view ***/audibility ***/a-c ** /heat **/assistance to carry disabled to seats (notify management in advance)/one buffet restaurant with bookable tables (tel: 858 1318)/two bars/performances: 7.45pm Mon-Sat/2.30 Sat.

Opened in 1969 in the renovated Victorian shell of Crowder's Music Hall, the Grenwich, under Ewan Hooper's dynamic management, began staging a series of classical revivals and new dramatic works which quickly earned the theatre a reputation as an important first venue for future West End productions. Among the Greenwich's many successful transfers are John Mortimer's *Voyage 'Round My Father*, Alan Ayckborn's *Norman Conquests*

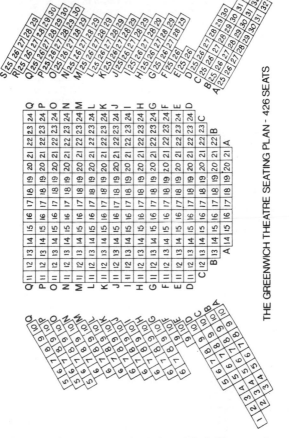

THE GREENWICH THEATRE SEATING PLAN - 426 SEATS

trily, and most recently Julian Mitchell's award-winning drama, *Another Country*.

BOOKING

£1.75-£6.00/concessions: OAPs, students, unemployed (standby only), groups of 10 or more/telephone booking: pay within 3 days of making reservation/postal booking: cheques to 'Greenwich Theatre Ltd.', include SAE/ credit cards: Visa-Barclaycard, Access-Mastercard, Diners' Club.

GETTING THERE

buses 108B, 177, 180, 185, 188 to Greenwich Theatre (or nearest stop); theatre at intersection of Crooms Hill and

Nevada Street, beside the National Maritime Museum.

British Rail Greenwich Station; Southern Regions lines leave every 30 minutes from Cannon Street, Charing Cross, Waterloo East and London Bridge. Last return train from Greenwich Station to central London, 11.33pm. From Greenwich Station walk left along Greenwich High Road to car park at Stockwell Street, theatre visible approx. 50 yards away.

boat Greenwich Pier; Regular daytime (only) boat trips from Westminister, Charing Cross, and Tower piers. From Greenwich pier walk up King William Walk approx. 900 yards to theatre.

HALF MOON THEATRE

213 Mile End Road E1 7AA
Map refs: SF 63 T12, A-Z 64 A1
Box Office: 790 4000 (10am-8pm Mon-Sat)

Fringe (plays, musicals)/flexible raked seating/open acting area/capacity 338/view ***/audibility ***/a-c: none/heat ***/wheelchair access, adapted rest-rooms/snacks/one bar/friendly pub next door/extras; cabaret, concerts, writers' workshops, East End Festival/Performances: 7.30pm or 8.00pm Mon-Sat.

Opened in a converted synagogue in 1972 as a permanent venue for political and alternative theatre in the East End, the Half Moon has proved to be one of the London's

Seating plan:

EAST UPPER GALLERY
1 2 3 4 5 6 7 8 9
WEST
1 2 3
EAST LOWER GALLERY
1 2 3 4 5 6 7 8 9
GALLERY
4 5 6

Rows (left to right: seats 1–6, row letter, seats 7 onward):

M 7 8 9 10 11 12 13 14 15 16 17 18 19 20 21 22 23 24 25 26
L 7 8 9 10 11 12 13 14 15 16 17 18 19 20 21 22 23 24 L
K 7 8 9 10 11 12 13 14 15 16 17 18 19 20 21 22 23 24 K
J 7 8 9 10 11 12 13 14 15 16 17 18 19 20 21 22 23 J
I 7 8 9 10 11 12 13 14 15 16 17 18 19 20 21 22 23 24 I
H 7 8 9 10 11 12 13 14 15 16 17 18 19 20 21 22 23 24 H
G 7 8 9 10 11 12 13 14 15 16 17 18 19 20 21 22 23 G
F 7 8 9 10 11 12 13 14 15 16 17 18 19 20 21 22 23 24 F
E 7 8 9 10 11 12 13 14 15 16 17 18 19 20 21 22 23 24 E
D 7 8 9 10 11 12 13 14 15 16 17 18 19 20 21 22 23 24 D
C 7 8 9 10 11 12 13 14 15 16 17 18 19 20 21 22 23 24 C
B 7 8 9 10 11 12 13 14 15 16 17 18 19 20 21 22 23 24 B
A 7 8 9 10 11 12 13 14 15 16 17 18 19 20 21 22 23 24 A

liveliest and most successful fringe theatres, staging a mixture of new works, classical revivals and musicals, plus serving as a community centre for all sorts of theatre-related, young people's workshops. The theatre also serves as a major venue for the East End Festival of art, drama and music.

BOOKING

£2.50-£5.00/concessions: OAPs, students, unemployed/ telephone booking: pay within three days of making reservation/postal booking: cheques to 'Half Moon Theatre', include SAE or collect at box office/credit cards: Visa-Barclaycard, Access-Mastercard.

GETTING THERE

buses 10, 25, 106, 225, 277, D1 to Stepney Green Station; from Stepney Green Station walk east across Globe Road, continue approx. 50 yards, theatre on left.

underground *District Line, Metropolitan Line* to Stepney Green; turn left out of station into Mile End Road, cross Globe Road, continue approx. 50 yards, theatre on left.

HAMPSTEAD THEATRE

Swiss Cottage Centre, Avenue Road NW3 3EX
Map refs: SF 130 F1, A-Z 44 A2
Box Office: 722 9301 (10am-8pm Mon-Sat)

Fringe (plays)/opened raked seating/platform end stage/ capacity 173/view ***/audibility ***/a-c **/heat ***/ wheelchair access, adapted rest-rooms/one bar-coffee bar/ performances: 8pm Mon-Sat/4.30pm Sat.

Probably the best known and certainly the most influential of London's smaller fringe theatres, the Hampstead, which was founded in 1959, burst onto the theatre scene in 1960 with its productions of *The Room* and *The Dumb Waiter*, 2 short plays by a then almost wholly unknown writer named Pinter. 3 years later, in new quarters, the Hampstead pulled off another *coup* with the London première of Laurie Lee's *Cider With Rosie*. Today, under the management of Michael Attenborough, the theatre continues to follow its original policy—6-to-8 week runs of the best new plays being written, all of them individually cast, and all of them eminently well worth seeing.

BOOKING

£1.20-£7.00/concessions: OAPs, students, unemployed, Camden Leisurecard holders, members (box office for details)/telephone booking; pay within three days of making reservation/postal booking: cheques to 'Hampstead Theatre', include SAE/credit cards: none/Club membership required (box office for details).

GETTING THERE

buses 2B, 13, 31, 46, 113, c11 to Swiss Cottage; exit in Avenue Road, theatre a few yards away beside library.

underground *Jubilee Line* to Swiss Cottage; directions as for Swiss Cottage buses

HAYMARKET—See Theatre Royal, Haymarket.

HER MAJESTY'S THEATRE

Haymarket SW1Y 4QR
Map refs: SF 140 F12, A-Z 60d D4
Box Office: 930 4025, 930 4026 (10am-8pm Mon-Sat)
Credit card booking: 930 6606, 930 6607, 930 2046, 930 2856
Stage Door: 930 6435

Mainstream (plays, musicals)/traditional auditorium/ proscenium stage/capacity 1260/view ** (some restricted seats in stalls and dress circle)/audibility ***/a-c */heat ***/ wheelchair space/three bars/performance times vary with production: see press.

The first of four theatres on this famous site was built by Sir John Vanbrugh in 1705. The present theatre, built by C.J. Phipps in 1897 for Sir Herbert Beerbohm Tree, is one of the most impressive Victorian theatre buildings ever conceived, let alone realized—justly described by historian John Earl as a 'magificent pile in the French Renaissance style', and well worth braving the traffic that roars continually down the Haymarket to get a good view from the far side, (especially at night). The interior, equally impressive, is modelled on the opéra at Versailles, and the huge proscenium arch, nearly 9 metres high, is a wonder of decorative engineering. High points in the present theatre's illustrious history include Tree's spectacular stagings of Shakespeare, (his *Midsummer Night's Dream* in 1900 featured a stage carpeted with real grass across which live rabbits cavorted); a then record-breaking, 2238-performance run of the oriental fantasy-musical *Chu-Chin-Chow* beginning in 1916; the first ever performance of Shaw's *Pygmalion*; and following World War II, a 4-year, non-stop run of Leonard Bernstein's *West Side Story*. Today, the theatre remains a leading home in London for the production of major musicals.

BOOKING

Telephone booking: pay within three days of making reservation/postal booking: cheques to 'Her Majesty's Theatre', include SAE/credit cards: Visa-Barclaycard, Access-Mastercard, American Express.

GETTING THERE

buses 3, 6, 9, 12, 13, 14, 15, 19, 22, 23, 38, 53, 55, 88, 159 to Piccadilly Circus (or any stop in Haymarket); walk down

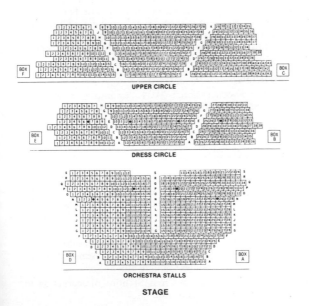

UPPER CIRCLE

DRESS CIRCLE

ORCHESTRA STALLS

STAGE

Haymarket approx. 250 yards, theatre on right. 1, 24, 29, 77, 77A, 170, 172, 176 to Trafalgar Square; Pall Mall East, right into Haymarket, theatre on left a few yards along.

underground *Bakerloo Line, Piccadilly Line* to Piccadilly Circus; Haymarket exit, down Haymarket approx. 250 yards, theatre on right.

British Rail Charing Cross Station; Strand exit to Trafalgar Square, continue as for Trafalgar Square buses.

ICA THEATRE

Nash House, Carlton Terrace, The Mall SW1Y 5AH
Map refs: SF 140 14F, A-Z 62d D1
Box Office: 930 3647 (Noon-8pm Tues-Sun)

Fringe (plays, performance)/flexible raked seating/flexible stage (thrust, platform, in-the-round)/capacity 210/ view ***/audibility ***/a-c **/heat ***/wheelchair access (no access to rest-rooms)/one restaurant/one bar/extras: cinema, bookshop, art gallery/performances: 8pm Tues-Sun.
Founded in 1947 and housed in John Nash's graceful, late Georgian Carlton House Terrace in the Mall, the Institute of Contemporary Arts opened its theatre in 1973, quickly establishing it as a centre for new and experimental works, both English and foreign, with an emphasis on political and social topics. In recent years a number of plays especially relevant to the women's movement have been staged with great success. Productions are always lively and provocative, and the atmosphere at the ICA is rarely less than enthusiastic.

BOOKING

£2.00-£4.50/concessions: OAPs, unemployed/telephone booking: pay within three days of making reservation/ postal booking: cheques to 'ICA Theatre', include SAE or collect at box office/credit cards: Visa-Barclaycard, Access-Mastercard, Diners' Club/Membership required: one day 60 pence; £12.00 per year; students £6.00 per year.

GETTING THERE

buses 1, 3, 6, 9, 11, 12, 13, 15, 23, 24, 29, 53, 77, 77A, 88, 159, 170, 172, 176 to Trafalgar Square; walk through Admiralty Arch into The Mall (north side), continue for approx. 200 yards, theatre on right.

underground *Bakerloo Line, Jubilee Line, Northern Line* to Charing Cross Station; Strand exit to Admiralty Arch, continue as for Trafalgar Square bus.

British Rail Charing Cross Station; directions as for Charing Cross underground.

JEANNETTA COCHRANE THEATRE

Southampton Row WC1B 4AP
Map refs: SF 140 M2, A-Z 60d F2
Box Office: 242 7040 (10am-8pm Mon-Fri)
Stage Door: 405 9184

Fringe-mainstream (plays, children's shows)/traditional auditorium/proscenium stage/capacity 351/view **/audibility **/a-c **/heat **/wheelchair access and seating (notify management in advance)/one bar/performances: 7.00 or 7.30pm Mon-Sun (variable).

Opened in 1965 as an extension of the Central School of Art and Design, the modern, purpose-built Cochrane theatre is now used as a professional venue for visiting companies staging both classical and new works, and it can be hired for filming, music, rehearsals etc.

BOOKING

Contact Box Office—variable with company performing/concessions: OAPs, children, parties of 10+ (variable with company performing)/telephone booking: pay within

Seating plan — BALCONY and STALLS, FORESTAGE

three days of making reservation/postal booking: cheques to individual theatre company (contact box office), include SAE or collect at box office/credit cards: variable with company (contact Box Office).

GETTING THERE

buses 5, 7, 8, 19, 22, 25, 38, 55, 68, 77A, 172, 188, 501 to Southampton Row at Theobald's Road; theatre located in modern wing of Central School of Art and Design at south-east corner of Southampton Row and Theobald's Road.

underground *Central Line, Piccadilly Line* to Holborn; walk up Southampton Row to Theobald's Road, continue as for Southampton Row buses.

KING'S HEAD PUB THEATRE

115 Upper Street, Islington, N1 1QN
Map refs: SF 133 W4, A-Z 46 3B
Booking: 226 1916 (10.30am-8pm)

Fringe (plays, new and revised musicals, thematic revue and cabaret)/club seating + open raked seating section/ platform stage/capacity 100 (30 at tables)/view ***/ audibility ***/a-c: none/heat **/wheelchair access, (notify management in advance)/full pub facilities and, for those dining in theatre, dinner begins 7pm/performances: 8pm Mon-Sat, lunchtime matinées 1.15pm, occasional late night cabaret 11.15pm Thurs-Sat (membership 50p).

One of London's most popular lunch and dinner theatre clubs, the King's Head theatre was founded in 1970 as a local Islington venue for staging new plays and neglected classics. Production bias is toward non-naturalistic material, particularly involving music. The back room theatre features mixed seating—tables for those who fancy dinner with their performance, ordinary seating for those just watching.

BOOKING

£5.00 (performance only) late night and lunchtime £2-£9.50 with dinner/concessions: student standby/ telephone booking: collect ticket 15 minutes in advance/ postal booking: cheques to, Kings Head Theatre Club', include SAE only if booking well in advance/credit cards: none.

GETTING THERE

buses 4, 19, 30, 43, 104, 172, 279, 279A to St. Mary's Church stop, Upper Street; pub directly across from St. Mary's Church.

underground *Northern Line* to Angel; walk north through Angel multiple intersection to Upper Street, continue, remembering to bear ½ left at Essex Road juction, to St. Mary's church, pub directly opposite. (6-8 minute walk). *Waterloo and City Line* to Essex Road; turn right from station, down Essex Road, right in St. Mary's Path to Upper Street, theatre opposite. (3-5 minute walk). *Victoria Line, Waterloo and City Line* to Highbury and Islington; Upper Street exit, walk down Upper Street approx. ½ mile to St. Mary's church, theatre opposite. (6-8 minute walk).

LATCHMERE THEATRE

503 Battersea Park Road, Battersea SW11 3BW
Map refs: SF 88 K4, A-Z 76 B2
Box Office: 228 2620 (10am-8pm Mon-Sat)

Fringe (plays)/fixed raked seating/platform stage/capacity 92/view ***/audibility **/a-c ***/heat ***/disabled facilities: none/one bar/extras: art exhibitions, some daytime performances, play readings/performances: 7.45pm Mon-Sat/10.15pm Fri-Sat

Purpose-built in 1982 and known originally as the Gate, the Latchmere Theatre opened promisingly with a 3-month, sellout run of *Fear and Loathing in Las Vegas* by Hunter S. Thompson, which then enjoyed another 3-month run at the Fortune Theatre in the West End. Since then, the Latchmere has continued to operate as a venue for top touring companies, as well as for its own resident company, staging new works and classical revivals of all kinds so long as their production standards are of the highest quality.

BOOKING

£2.00/concessions: OAPs, students, unemployed, groups of 10 or more/telephone booking: arrange details with box office/postal booking: cheques to 'Latchmere Theatre', include SAE or collect at box office/credit cards: Visa-Barclaycard, Access-Mastercard, Diners' Club, American Express.

GETTING THERE

buses 19, 39, 44, 45, 170, 249 to Latchmere Road (Junction of Battersea Bridge Road and Battersea Park Road); theatre just a few yards away at intersection—look for 503 Battersea Park Road. 37, 77, 77A, 156, 249, 295 to Clapham Junction; walk up Falcon Road approx. 600 yards, right into Battersea Park Road, theatre at intersection with Latchmere Road.

British Rail Clapham Junction; directions as for Clapham Junction buses.

LONDON COLISEUM

St. Martin's Lane WC2N 4ES
Map refs: SF 140 J10, A-Z 60d E4
Box Office: 836 3161 (10am-8pm Mon-Sat)
Credit card booking: 240 5258, 379 6433
Recorded Information: 836 7666
Group booking: 836 0111 ext 318

Mainstream (opera)/traditional auditorium/proscenium stage/capacity 2358/view *** (2 obstructed seats—sold last)/audibility *** (but some difficulty at back of circles/a-c

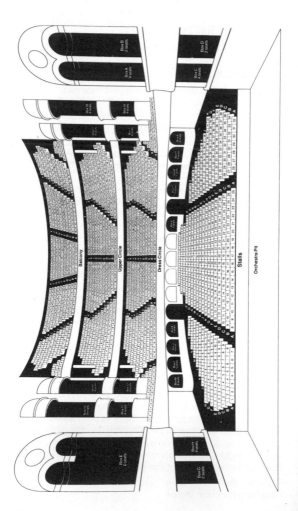

**/heat **/wheelchair access to some boxes, rest-rooms adapted for disabled (notify management in advance on 836 0111 ext. 329)/ two supper bars with bookable tables/ two buffet bars/four bars/extras: lunchtime recitals at 1.05pm in Terrace Bar, ocasional pre-perfomance lectures at Friends' Meeting House in St Martin's Lane/ performances: 7pm or 7.30pm Mon-Sat.

Conceived as a magnificent variety hall in 1904 by the foremost theatre designer of his day, Frank Matcham, the huge London Coliseum with its splendid Romanesque façade, soaring globe-topped tower, and opulent interior detail probably remains the most luxurious and indulgently comfortable theatre ever built in London. The home first of spectacular variety entertainment, then spectacular musicals, the Coliseum has been since 1968 the permanent residence of the English National Opera Company.

BOOKING
£4.00-£18.50/concessions: contact box office/telephone booking: pay within 3 days of making reservation/postal booking: cheques to 'English National Opera', include SAE/credit cards: Visa-Barclaycard, Access-Mastercard, Diners' Club, American Express.

GETTING THERE
buses 1, 24, 29, 176 to Leicester Square; walk down Charing Cross Road (downhill) to top of St. Martin's Place, sharp left around corner into St. Martin's Lane, theatre on right a few yards along. 3, 6, 9, 11, 12, 13, 15, 23, 53, 77, 77A, 88, 159, 170, 172 to Trafalgar Square; walk uphill through St. Martin's Place, bear ½ right into St. Martin's lane, theatre on right a few yards along. 14, 19, 38, 55 to Cambridge Circus; walk down Charing Cross Road (downhill to top of St. Martin's Place, sharp left around corner into St. Martin's Lane, theatre on right a few yards along.

underground *Piccadilly Line, Northern Line* to Leicester Square; Charing Cross Road East exit, continue as for Leicester Square buses. *Bakerloo Line, Jubilee Line* to Charing Cross Station; Strand exit to Trafalgar Square, continue as for Trafalgar Square buses.

British Rail Charing Cross Station; directions as for Charing Cross underground.

LONDON PALLADIUM

Argyll Street W1A 3AB
Map refs: SF 140 A6, A-Z 60c B3
Box office: 437 7373, 437 2055 (10am-8pm)
Stage door: 437 1278

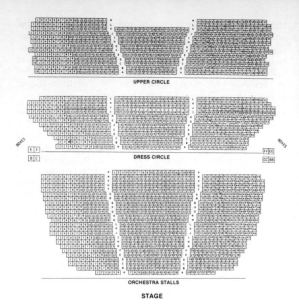

UPPER CIRCLE

DRESS CIRCLE

ORCHESTRA STALLS

STAGE

Mainstream (musicals, variety, revue, pantomime, concerts) / traditional auditorium / proscenium stage / capacity 2317/view ***/audibility ***/a-c */heat ***/wheelchair access (notify management in advance)/four bars/ performance times vary with production: see press.

Built in 1910 as a rival variety theatre to the Coliseum, the London Palladium's painted stone façade is modelled on a classical temple, while its interior represents yet another Frank Matcham triumph in the art of lavish neo-Renaissance theatre decoration. For many years London's most prestigious variety theatre, ('playing the Palladium' was for variety enterainers what playing the Met or La Scala is for opera singers), the theatre is now used mainly for spectacular revues, big musicals and Christmas pantomimes.

BOOKING

Postal booking: cheques to 'London Palladium', include SAE/credit cards: Visa-Barclaycard, Access-Mastercard, American Express.

GETTING THERE

buses 1, 3, 6, 7, 8, 12, 13, 15, 16A, 23, 25, 53, 73, 88, 113, 137, 159, 500 to Oxford Circus; walk down Regent Street (keeping Dickens and Jones department store on left), left into Little Argyll Street, theatre opposite in Argyll Street.

underground *Bakerloo Line, Central Line, Victoria Line* to Oxford Circus; Argyll Street exit; theatre 150 yards on left.

LYRIC THEATRE

Shaftesbury Avenue W1V 8ES
Map refs: SF 140 E9, A-Z 60d D3
Box Office: 437 3686, 437 3687, 434 1050 (10am-8pm Mon-Sat)
Credit card booking: 434 1550, 734 5166, 734 5167
Stage door: 437 5443

Mainstream (plays, musicals)/traditional auditorium/proscenium stage/capacity 961/view ** (some restricted seats in dress circle and stalls)/audibility ***/a-c */heat ***/wheelchair access/four bars/performance times vary with production: see press.

Westernmost and architecturally most unusual of the four, grouped Shaftesbury Avenue theatres, the Lyric, built in 1888 by C.J. Phipps, resembles nothing so much as an important Dutch townhouse with a sensible glass canopy protecting its entrance. The handsome rather than elaborate interior carries forward a kind of Delft motif, and the whole effect, as one might expect in a prosperous burgher's home, is welcoming, cosy, somewhat dusty and extremely comfortable. The same degree of comfort marks the theatre's history; being largely a chronicle of consistently successful operettas, musicals, classical revivals, 'good' comedies and serious (but not *too* serious) new dramas. Nothing really spectacular has ever happened at the Lyric, but then nothing really disasterous

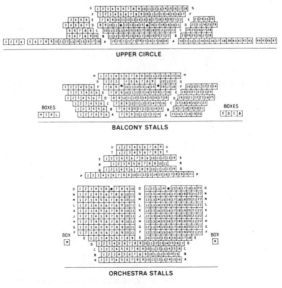

UPPER CIRCLE

BALCONY STALLS

ORCHESTRA STALLS

STAGE

has ever happened either. There are no ghosts, no tales of violence, and the theatre's longest run, a solid 1261 performances, was of a play almost no one remembers called *The Little Hut*.

BOOKING

Postal booking: cheques to 'Lyric Theatre', include SAE/ credit cards: Visa-Barclaycard, Access-Mastercard, American Express.

GETTING THERE

buses 1, 14, 19, 22, 24, 29, 38, 55, 176 to Cambridge Circus (or nearest stop in Shaftesbury Avenue to Wardour Street); from all stops, look for theatre at the west (downhill) end of the group of four theatres on the north side of Shaftesbury Avenue approx. half-way between Cambridge Circus and Piccadilly Circus. 3, 6, 9, 12, 13, 15, 23, 53, 88, 159 to Piccadilly Circus; to Shaftesbury Avenue and continue as for Cambridge Circus buses.

underground *Bakerloo Line, Piccadilly Line* to Piccadilly Circus; Shaftesbury Avenue exit and continue as for Cambridge Circus buses. *Northern Line* to Leicester Square; Cranbourn Street to Leicester Square, walk through Square, right in Wardour Street to Shaftesbury Avenue, continue as for Cambridge Circus buses.

LYRIC THEATRE, HAMMERSMITH

King Street, Hammersmith W6 0QL
Map refs: SF 144 B7, A-Z 58 C4
Box Office: 741 2311 (10am-7pm Mon-Sat)
Credit card booking: 741 2311

Main Theatre Mainstream (plays, musicals, performance)/traditional auditorium/proscenium stage/ capacity 530/view ** (restricted view seats sold last)/ audibility ***/a-c **/heat **/wheelchair access and seating, hearing loops, adapted rest rooms, (notify management in advance). Performances: 7.45pm Mon-Sat/2.30pm Wed/4pm Sat.
Studio Theatre Fringe (plays, performance)/flexible raked seating/open acting area/capacity 110/view ***/audibility ** */a-c */heat */wheelchair access, but must fold chairs and sit on benches, (notify management in advance). Performances: 8pm Mon-Sat.
Both theatres One buffet restaurant (after-show suppers, book in advance through Catering Dept.)/three bars.

The original Lyric Hammersmith, (built in 1888), burnt down in 1965 and was then rebuilt in 1979 following Frank Matcham's 1895 interior designs and employing as much of the original Victorian plasterwork as could be

Main House Seating Plan

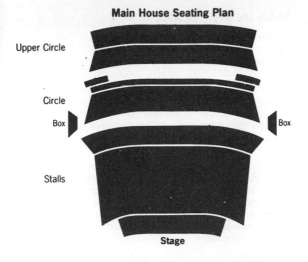

Upper Circle

Circle

Box   Box

Stalls

Stage

rehabilitated. Housed in a modern building off Hammersmith Broadway, the faithful 'Matcham restoration' is the home of an active and enthusiastic local theatre community which supports West End productions, classical revivals, and a variety of new works. The Lyric Studio, which stages mainly experimental and foreign plays, enjoys the same degree of community support; and while the theatre complex is some distance from central London, the journey is in nearly every case well worth the extra time required getting there.

BOOKING

£5.00-£10.00/concessions: OAPs, students, unemployed (standby tickets only), groups of 10 or more/telephone booking: pay within three working days of making reservation/postal booking: cheques to 'Lyric Theatre, Hammersmith', include SAE or collect at box office/credit cards: Visa-Barclaycard, Access-Mastercard, Diners' Club, American Express.

GETTING THERE

buses   9, 11, 27, 33, 72, 73, 91, 220, 260, 266, 267, 283, 290, 295, 701, 704, 710, 714, 715, 730, 740, X12 to Hammersmith Broadway; theatre on right approx. 50 yards along King Street.

underground   *District Line, Metropolitan Line, Piccadilly Line* to Hammersmith; Hammersmith Broadway (King Street) exit, continue as for Hammersmith Broadway buses.

MAN IN THE MOON

392 Kings Road, Chelsea SW3 5UZ
Map refs: SF 146 F15, A-Z 76 A1
Booking: 351 2876.
Information: 351 5701.

Fringe (plays)/newly refurbished/fixed raked comfortable seating on two sides with upper gallery/capacity 64/view excellent/audibility ***/a-c: none/heat **/disabled facilities by prior arrangement/pub close by/performances: two different shows nightly. Tues-Sun, usually 7.30pm and 9.45pm. Please phone to confirm.

One of London's best known pub theatres (located, actually, in converted cold-storage warehouse at the back), the Man in the Moon maintains a policy of staging both new plays and neglected works of the 1960s and 70s, with special emphasis on adaptations from non-theatrical sources and one and two-hand performances, especially in the late-night slot.

BOOKING

£1.50-£3.50/concessions: OAPs, students, unemployed/ group reductions by prior arrangement.

GETTING THERE

buses   11, 19, 22, 45, 49 to Kings Road to Beaufort Street; Man in the Moon pub visible just a few yards away.

underground   *District or Circle Line* to Sloane Square: walk down Kings Road approx. 1 mile to Beaufort Street, or catch buses 11, 19, 22.

MAYFAIR THEATRE

Mayfair Hotel, Stratton Street W1A 2AN
Map refs: SF 139 Z13, A-Z 60c 4B
Box Office: 629 3036, 629 3037 (advance booking) (10am-8pm Mon-Sat)
Credit card booking: 629 3036, 741 9999

Mainstream (plays)/open raked seating/proscenium stage/capacity 310/view ***/audibility ***/a-c ***/heat ***/ wheelchair access (notify management in advance/one restaurant/one coffee-shop/two bars/all hotel facilities/ performances: 8.00pm Mon-Thurs/5.40pm & 8.10pm Fri-Sat.

Originally the Candlelight Ballroom of the Mayfair Hotel, (famous as the home of big band radio broadcasts in the 1930s), the management installed a beautifully equipped proscenium stage in 1963 and the ballroom began its new life as a theatre with a highly successful production, starring Ralph Richardson, of Pirandello's *Six Characters in*

Search of an Author. Since then the theatre has remained one of London's most popular venues for the staging of new and experimental works as well as revivals of modern classics. Christopher Hampton's *The Philanthropist* ran here for nearly 1000 performances in the 1970s, and Richard Harris's eccentric thriller *The Business of Murder* was in its fifth year at time of writing.

BOOKING

£7.00-£9.50/concessions: OAPs, students (standby), groups of 20 or more/telephone booking: pay within 3 days of making reservation/postal booking: cheques to 'Mayfair Theatre', include SAE/credit cards: Visa-Barclaycard, Access-Mastercard, Diners' Club, American Express.

GETTING THERE

buses 9, 14, 19, 22, 25, 38, 55 to Green Park (Berkeley Street at Piccadilly); walk down Piccadilly 1 block, right into Stratton Street, hotel within a few yards. 3, 6, 12, 13, 15, 23, 53, 88, 159 to Piccadilly Circus; walk down Piccadilly approx. 800 yards, right into Stratton Street, hotel within a few yards.

underground *Piccadilly Line, Jubilee Line, Victoria Line* to Green Park; exit at Stratton Street and Piccadilly, theatre a few yards away. *Bakerloo Line* to Piccadilly Circus; Piccadilly exit, continue as for Piccadilly Circus buses.

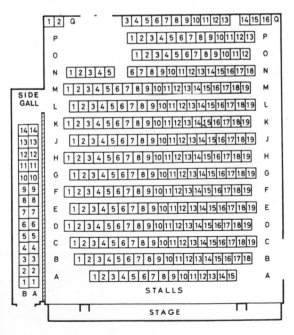

MERMAID THEATRE

Puddle Dock, Blackfriars EC4V 3DD
Map refs: SF 141 X9, A-Z 61a C3
Box Office: 236 5568 (10am-8pm Mon-Sat)
Credit card booking: 236 5568, 741 9999
Group booking: 930 6123

Fringe/Mainstream (plays)/open plan auditorium/open end stage/capacity 610/view ***/audibility ***/a-c ***/ heat ***/two bars/wheelchair seating/lifts/hearing loops/ disabled rest-rooms/one buffet/two bars/performances: 8.30pm Mon-Fri and 6 + 8.30pm Sat.

One of London's most influential venues for the staging of new works and classical revivals, the Mermaid originated in 1945 as a private theatre built on the Elizabethan model by actor-manager Sir Bernard Miles in a hall attached to his St. John's Wood home. The theatre then moved to temporary public premises at Puddle Dock in 1951, and into its permanent home in the Mermaid Conference and Exhibition Centre on the same site in 1981. Throughout its history the Mermaid has been renowned for its high production standards and careful attention to the purity of dramatic presentation.

BOOKING

£6.00-£9.00/concessions: OAPs, students, unemployed/

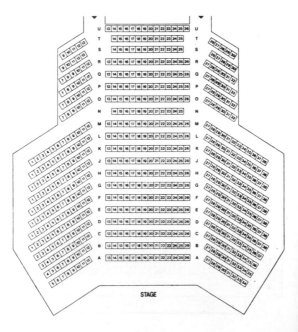

telephone booking: pay within 3 working days of making reservation (or make special arrangement with box office)/postal booking: cheques to 'Mermaid Theatre', include SAE/credit cards: Visa-Barclaycard, Access-Mastercard, American Express.

GETTING THERE

buses 45, 63, 76, 109, 141, 155, 184 to Blackfriars Station; walk a few yards along Queen Victoria Street, right into Puddle Dock, theatre straight ahead. 4, 6, 9, 11, 15, 18, 23, 45, 63, 76, 77, 141, 502, 513 to Ludgate Circus; walk down New Bridge Street to Blackfriars Station, continue as for Blackfriars buses.

underground *District or Circle Line* to Blackfriars; directions as for Blackfriars buses.

British Rail Blackfriars Station; directions as for Blackfriars buses.

NATIONAL THEATRE

South Bank SE1 9PX
Map refs: SF 141 Y R13, A-Z 61a A4
Box Office: 928 2252 (10am-8pm Mon-Sat)
Credit card booking: as above
Booking information: 928 8126 (24-hr, recorded)
General information: 633 0880 (10am-11pm daily)
Stage door: 928 2033

Olivier Theatre Mainstream (plays, musicals)/open-plan auditorium/open platform stage/capacity 1160/view ***/audibility ***/a-c ***/heat ***/wheelchair access and seating, ramps and lifts/front-row seating for hard of hearing/disabled rest-rooms (notify management in advance).

Lyttelton Theatre · Mainstream (plays)/traditional auditorium (continental design)/proscenium stage/capacity 890/view ***/audibility ***/a-c ***/heat ***/wheelchair access and seating, ramps and lifts/front-row seating for hard of hearing/disabled rest-rooms (notify management in advance).

Cottesloe Theatre Fringe (plays, musicals)/arena gallery seating, plus flexible flat floor seating/flexible platform stage, adaptable to open acting area/capacity 400/view ***/audibility ***/a-c ***/heat ***/disabled facilities: none.

All theatres One restaurant, 'Orations', open lunchtime and 5.30pm-12.30am (last orders 11pm); reservations: 928 2033 ext 531 (day), ext 561 (ev)/four buffet restaurants/six bars/extras: music recitals in the foyer and outdoors, art exhibitions and bookshops/performance times vary with productions: check with Box Office.

Olivier Auditorium

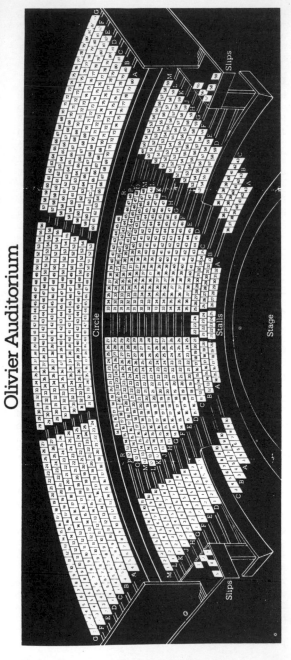

Circle

Slips

Slips

Stalls

Stage

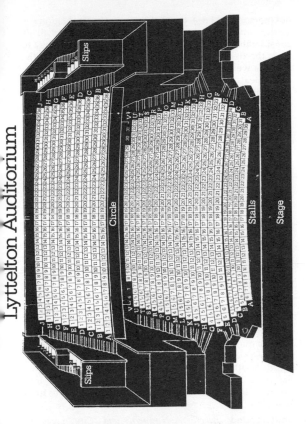

Lyttelton Auditorium

Three theatres—the Olivier, the Lyttelton and the
Cottesloe—all housed in one building of London's huge
South Bank Complex, have served as the permanent
home of the National Theatre company since 1976. The
largest of the three, the Olivier, with its circular open stage
and fan-shaped open-plan auditorium, is ideally suited to
large, spectacular productions of all kinds.

The traditionally-designed, 890-seat Lyttelton, with its
proscenium stage and finely-engineered two-tier seating,
provides a perfect setting for classical revivals and modern
works of drama. And the Cottesloe, smallest and most
flexible of the three, with seating and acting space
modelled on the Elizabethan inn yards where Londoners
first saw plays over 300 years ago, offers an ideal venue for
experimental works.

The South Bank's architecture, all glass and soaring
concrete slabs on a mammoth scale, has, like the
Barbican's interior design, given rise to some heated
discussion over the years. But whether you like the look or

not (personally, I do), the buildings work. The National is neither intimidating nor confusing to enter, for all its considerable size, everything is well signed and easy to find, the décor is restful, the furniture comfortable, the space is well and humanely used, and—best of all—the three theatres are splendidly designed for good viewing, audibility and access.

As for the history and reputation of the National Theatre Company, all one needs to say is that, along with the RSC, it remains the finest theatrical repertory company in the English-speaking world.

BOOKING

£5.50-£12.50/concessions: OAPs, students, unemployed, some disabled, groups of 12-plus, standbys/telephone booking: pay within three working days of making reservation/postal booking: cheques to 'National Theatre', include SAE/credit cards: Visa-Barclaycard, Access-Mastercard, Diners' Club, American Express.

GETTING THERE

buses 1, 4, 5, 68, 70, 76, 149, 171, 176, 177, 188, 501, 502, 507, 513 to Waterloo Station or Waterloo Bridge; from all stops walk towards river, crossing York Road, and continue towards South Bank Complex until you pick up signs to National Theatre. Main entrances are on river side of building. Box Office entrance is at the far right as you face the main entrances. Cottesloe entrance is around the left-hand side of the building, approx. 50 yards along. 45, 63, 70, 76, 109, 141, 149, 155 to Stamford Street; walk down Stamford Street approx. 500 yards, then right into Cornwall Road, cross Upper Ground and continue as from Waterloo.

underground *Bakerloo, Northern and City Lines* to Waterloo Station; turn left out of main entrance, then proceed as above.

British Rail Trains to Waterloo Station, then as from underground.

NEW END THEATRE—Reopening after closure: phone 794 0022 or 794 0023 for information.

NEW INN THEATRE

The New Inn, St. Mary's Road, Ealing W5
Map refs: SF 72 G5-6, A-Z 56 B3
Booking: 567 8352 (Noon-8pm Wed-Sun

Fringe (plays)/pews with cushions/open acting area/ capacity 40/view *** /audibility ***/a-c: none/heat **/

disabled facilities: none/full pub facilities downstairs, hot meals lunch and evening until 8pm/performances: usually 7.45pm Wed-Sun.

A small pub theatre catering mainly to the Ealing community, the New Inn leans toward established playwrights with an emphasis on American drama of a thought-provoking but not excessively controversial nature.

BOOKING

£3.00-£3.75/concessions: OAPs, students, unemployed £2.00/telephone booking: collect-pay 15 minutes before performance/postal booking: cheques to 'New Inn Theatre', include SAE or collect tickets at door/credit cards: none.

GETTING THERE

buses 65 to St. Mary's Road (ask for New Inn Pub; stops right outside the door. 83, 112, 207, 273, 274 to Ealing Broadway (or nearest stop); walk south in The Broadway, continue down Ealing Green, on into St. Mary's Road and look for New Inn.

underground *Piccadilly Line (Heathrow branch)* to South Ealing; turn left and walk for five minutes.

NEW LONDON THEATRE

Drury Lane and Parker Street, WC2B 5PW
Map refs: SF 140 L5, A-Z 60d F2
Box Office: 405 0072 (10am-7.45pm Mon-Sat)
Credit card booking: 404 4079, 379 6131
Group booking: 405 1567, 930 6123
Stage Door: 242 9802

Mainstream (musicals)/open plan arena seating with circle/open platform stage/capacity 1106/view ***/ audibility ***/a-c **/heat ***/limited wheelchair access (notify management in advance)/one coffee-bar/two bars/ performances: 7.45pm Mon-Sat, 3pm Tues & Sat.

The New London, with its soaring glass facade and all-electric auditorium, (everything can be rearranged by pushing buttons—stage, seats, even the walls), remains exactly what it was called when it opened in 1973, 'the theatre of the future'. In its brief history the New London has had one early Peter Ustinov success, *The Unknown Soldier and his Wife*, has served as a television studio, and is now the home of Andrew Lloyd Webber's spectacular musical, *Cats*, already 5 years in residence and probably set for another 4 at least.

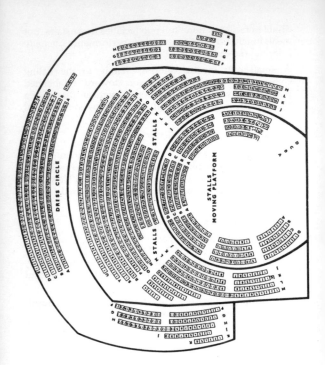

BOOKING

£7.00-£18.50/concessions: contact box office/telephone booking: pay within three days of making reservation/ postal booking: cheques to 'New London Theatre', include SAE (at time of writing, postal bookings were being accepted only three months in advance due to the phenomenal success of *Cats*)/credit cards: none.

GETTING THERE

buses   1, 4, 5, 6, 9, 11, 13, 15, 23, 68, 77, 77A, 170, 171, 172, 176, 188, 501, 502, 513 to Aldwych; walk up Drury Lane approx. 400 yards, theatre on right at corner of Parker Street. 7, 8, 19, 22, 25, 35, 55 to Holborn; walk down Kingsway, right into Parker Street, theatre at corner of Drury Lane. 14, 24, 29, 38 to Cambridge Circus; Earlham Street 2 blocks, cross Neal Street, continue on in Shelton Street to Drury Lane, theatre on right at corner of Parker Street.

underground   *Central Line*, *Piccadilly Line* to Holborn; directions as for Holborn buses. *Northern Line* to Leicester Square; Cranbourn Street to Long Acre, continue approx. 500 yards, left into Drury Lane, theatre on right at corner of Parker Street.

OFFSTAGE

37 Chalk Farm Road, Camden Town NW1 8AJ
Map refs: SF 47 R20, A-Z 45 D2
Booking: 267 9649 (10am-6pm Mon-Sat, 11am-5pm Sun)

Fringe (plays)/flexible raked seating/open acting area/ capacity 48-56/view ***/audibility ***/a-c */heat **/disabled facilities: none/one snack-bar/performances: 8pm Tues-Sun.

A studio theatre attached to the Offstage bookshop which specializes in small-scale productions of newly written works performed by both the resident and touring companies.

BOOKING

£3.25/concessions: students, unemployed/telephone booking: pay within five days of making reservation/ postal booking: cheques to 'Offstage Downstairs', include SAE or collect at door/credit cards: Visa-Barclaycard, Access-Mastercard only.

GETTING THERE

buses 31, 68 to Camden Lock (or nearest stop to Harmood Street; look for Offstage bookshop on north side of Chalk Farm Road facing Camden Lock. 3, 24, 27, 29, 53, 74, 134, 137, 214, 253 to Camden Town Station; walk uphill in Camden High Street approx. 400 yards to Camden Lock, look for Offstage bookshop on right.

underground *Northern Line* to Camden Town; directions as for Camden Town buses. *Northern Line* to Chalk Farm; walk down Chalk Farm Road approx. 400 yards, past Harmood Street, look for Offstage bookshop on left.

British Rail Trains to Primrose Hill; Regent's Park Road to Chalk Farm Road, turn right and continue as for Chalk Farm underground.

OLD RED LION THEATRE CLUB

St. John Street, Islington EC1V 4NJ
Map refs: SF 133 V10, A-Z 46 A4
Booking: 837 7816 (11am-8pm)

Fringe (plays)/fixed raked seating/open acting area/ capacity 70/view ***/audibility ***/a-c */heat **/disabled facilities: none/full pub facilities downstairs, hot meals/ extras: occasional play-readings and late night shows/ performances: 8pm Tues-Sun.

A popular pub theatre in trendy Islington, founding of the Old Red Lion is said by author Barry Turner (*The Playgoer's Companion*) to have been inspired in 1979 when the landlord and his wife, seeing how many actors drank there, suggested that they put on a show. They did, apparently, and the theatre has been thriving ever since, staging fine small productions of new plays and works not previously seen in London, several of which have transferred to larger theatres and one of which, Phil Young's *Crystal Clear*, moved to Wyndham's in 1983; the only fringe play I've heard of in recent years to make it directly from a pub to the West End in one spectacular leap.

BOOKING

£4/concessions: OAPs, students, unemployed/telephone booking: collect-pay fifteen minutes before performance/ postal booking: cheques to 'Old Red Lion Theatre Club', include SAE or collect at door, postal booking without payment okay/credit cards: none.

GETTING THERE

buses 4, 19, 30, 38, 43, 73, 153, 171, 214, 277, 279, 279A to Angel; look for back entrance to Old Red Lion pub just opposite Angel underground station, or front entrance in St John's Street 50 yards from traffic lights at Angel.

underground *Northern Line* to Angel; Old Red Lion pub back entrance just opposite station.

OLD VIC

Waterloo Road, Waterloo SE1 8NB
Map refs: SF 141 U17, A-Z 63a B1
Box Office: 928 7616 (10am-8pm Mon-Sat)
Credit card booking: 261 1821
Stage Door: 928 2651

Mainstream (plays and musicals)/traditional auditorium/ proscenium stage/capacity 1067/view ** (discount on restricted view tickets/audibility ***/a-c ***/heat ***/ wheelchair access, two wheelchair seating spaces, disabled rest-rooms (notify management in advance)/four bars (all service sandwiches, open 1hr before curtain)/ performances: 7.30pm Mon-Fri, 2.30pm Wed, 4pm + 7.45pm Sat.

Original home of the National Theatre Company and for much of the 20th Century the principal champion of serious classical drama in London, the Old Vic is more than just a theatre; it is, in the true sense of the word, an institution—and a most beloved one. Opened as The Royal Coburg in 1818, the imposing brick and stucco building was for many decades the somewhat disreputable home of low melodrama South of the river. Beginning late in the 19th Century the theatre served a stint as a temperance amusement hall; but in 1914, Lilian

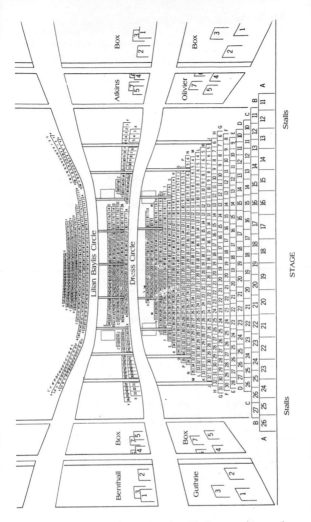

Baylis (see history) began staging Shakespeare's works there on a regular basis, and from that time until the South Bank Complex opened in 1976, if you wanted to see Shakespeare and other classics done properly, you either hunted up the RSC at one of its several theatres or you crossed the Thames to the Old Vic. (The name 'Old Vic', after Queen Victoria, is really only a nickname, though an official one now). After 1977 the theatre underwent hard times for awhile, but it has now been refurbished and is once more serving as a home for serious dramatic works and 'good' comedy.

BOOKING

£4.00-£12.50/concessions: OAPs, students, unemployed (all standby, 1 hour before performance)/advance booking office in Annexe adjacent to theatre, open 10am-6pm Mon-Sat/telephone booking: pay within four working days of making reservation/postal booking: cheques to 'The Old Vic', include SAE/credit cards: Visa-Barclaycard, Access-Mastercard, Diners' Club, American Express/ subscription seasons.

GETTING THERE

buses   1, 4, 5, 68, 70, 76, 149, 171, 176, 177, 188, 501, 502, 507, 513 to Waterloo Station; turn right out of station, walk down Waterloo Road to The Cut, theatre on corner on your left.

underground   *Bakerloo Line, Northern Line* to Waterloo; Directions as for Waterloo buses.

British Rail   Trains to Waterloo Sation; directions as for Waterloo buses.

OLIVIER — See NATIONAL THEATRE

OPEN AIR THEATRE, REGENT'S PARK

Inner Circle, Regent's Park NW1 4NU
Map refs: SF 131 S13-14, A-Z 44 C4
Box Office: 486 2431 (10am-6pm May-September)
Credit card booking: 379 6433, 486 1933
Stage Door: 486 6991

Mainstream (plays; seasons of Shakespeare)/open plan fan-shaped auditorium/circular platform stage/capacity 1187 (plus space on grass)/view ***/audibility ***/a-c provided by Mother Nature/heat: ditto/wheelchair access, adapted rest-rooms (notify management in advance)/one buffet-barbecue/one wine bar/picnic tables/performances: 7.45pm Mon-Sat, 2.30pm Wed-Thurs & Sat. (1 June-1 Sept)

Founded in 1933, the Open Air Theatre is now the resident home of the New Shakespeare Company, who stage, during the Summer months, spectacular productions of Shakespeare and occasionally other classics in the sylvan surrounding of Regent's Park. Amphitheatre seating was installed in 1974.

BOOKING

£3.50-£10.00/concessions: contact box office/telephone booking: collect-pay one hour before performance/postal booking: cheques to 'Open Air Theatre', include SAE/credit cards: Visa-Barclaycard, Access-Mastercard, American Express.

GETTING THERE

buses 18, 27, 30, 176 to Marylebone Road (nearest stop to York Gate); York Gate into Regent's Park, continue on to Queen Mary's Garden and follow sign posting through garden to theatre, or take Inner Circle around to your left until you come to theatre. 1, 2, 2B, 13, 74, 113, 159 to Baker Street Station; walk toward park in Baker Street, cross Park Road, enter park at Clarence Gate, right in Outer Circle, left across footbridge, follow sign posting to theatre, or walk left past Bedford College to Inner Circle and continue around to your left until you reach theatre. 3, 53, 137 to Great Portland Street Station; cross Marylebone Road, to Park Square East, left along Outer Circle to York Gate, continue as for Marylebone Road buses.

underground *Bakerloo Line* to Regent's Park; cross Marylebone to Park Square West, left along Outer Circle to York Gate, continue as for Marylebone Road buses. *Bakerloo Line, Circle Line, Jubilee Line, Metropolitan Line* to Baker Street; directions as for Baker Street buses.

ORANGE TREE

45 Kew Road, Richmond, Surrey
Map refs: SF 84 J10, A-Z 72 B3
Box Office: 940 3633 (10am-8pm Mon-Sat)

Fringe (plays)/theatre in the round/church pews/open acting area/capacity 80/view ***/audibility ***/a-c **/heat **/ theatre upstairs over pub/one restaurant in pub cellar (12-3pm, 6-12pm; tel. 940 0944 for reservations;)/full pub facilities/performances: 7.30pm or 8pm Mon-Sat, occasional matinées Wed and Sun.

Founded in 1971 by an enthusiastic group of actors, directors and writers, the Orange Tree pub theatre continues to mount excellent small productions of new, experimental and classic plays, and present shows for schools, for children and the elderly.

BOOKING

£2.50-£5/concessions: OAPs, students, unemployed, parents claiming child benefits/telephone booking: collect and pay just before performance/advance booking for groups only/postal booking: none/credit cards: none.

GETTING THERE

buses 7, 27, 65, 71, 90B, 202, 270, 290 to Kew Road at Lower Mortlake Road; theatre just a few yards along in Kew Road—look for Orange Tree pub.

underground *District Line* to Richmond; turn right into Quadrant, theatre approx 75 yards along.

British Rail Trains to Richmond Station; proceed as from underground.

OVAL HOUSE

52-54 Kennington Oval, SE11 5SW
Map refs: SF 149 P15, A-Z 77 E1
Box Office: 582 7680 (10am-8pm Wed-Sun)
Information: 735 2786, 582 7680 (answerphone)

Main Theatre (downstairs) Fringe (plays)/open auditorium/open acting area, flexible/capacity 100/ view *** (varies with stage arrangement)/audibility ***/a-c: none—warm in Summer/heat **/wheelchair access, hearing loops, downstairs rest-rooms adapted for disabled.

Studio Theatre (upstairs) Fringe (plays, workshops)/ open seating/open acting area, flexible/view ***/audibility ***/a-c: none—very hot in Summer/heat **/disabled facilities as for main theatre, (wheelchair access to studio impractical)/performances: 7.30pm Wed-Sun (main theatre), 8.30pm Wed-Sun (studio).

Originally a south London youth club located beside the Oval cricket ground, the Oval House became an arts centre in the late 1960s and began staging new and experimental plays in 2 newly equipped open plan studios. New, alternative, acting companies as well as older established groups are booked on a regular basis, and the Oval House has now become a leading supporter of the London fringe movement.

BOOKING

£1.50-£3.00/concessions: under-18/telephone booking: collect tickets thirty minutes before perrformance (held later on request); telephone booking also through Fringe Box Office, Duke of Yorks Theatre, St. Martin's Lane, tel: 379 6002 (they will accept credit cards)/postal booking: cheques to 'Oval House', include SAE/credit cards: (through Fringe Box Office only) Visa-Barclaycard, Access-Mastercard, Diners' Club, American Express.

GETTING THERE

buses 3, 36, 36A, 36B, 95, 109, 133, 159, 172, 185 to Surrey Tavern stop, Kennington Oval; theatre visible opposite cricket ground entry.

underground *Northern Line* to Oval; walk to Kennington Oval, theatre visible opposite cricket ground entry.

PALACE THEATRE

Shaftesbury Avenue W1V 8AY
Map refs: SF 140 G7-8, A-Z 60d D3
Box Office: 437 8329, 379 6433
Credit card booking: 930 6123
Group booking: 930 6123
Stage Door: 437 4144

Mainstream (musicals, traditional auditorium/
proscenium stage/capacity 1450/view ** (seats with
restricted views sold at lower prices)/audibility ***/a-c
none/heat ***/wheelchair access and seating and adapted
rest-rooms (notify management in advance)/one buffet
with hot food/four bars/performances: 7.30pm Mon-Sat +
2.30pm Thurs and Sat.

A genuinely monumental, Victorian-Renaissance palace
built for Richard D'Oyly Carte in 1891 as the future home
of grand opera in London (which it never became), the
Palace Theatre was once the architectural glory of
Cambridge Circus. It saw only one opera (Sir Arthur
Sullivan's *Ivanhoe*, which wasn't terribly good) and one
great actress (Sara Bernhardt, who was) before D'Oyly
Carte's dream evaporated, and the theatre turned
realistically to variety to keep afloat. Musicals became the
Palace's mainstay after 1925 and have remained so, with
consistent success, ever since. In 1961 *The Sound of Music*

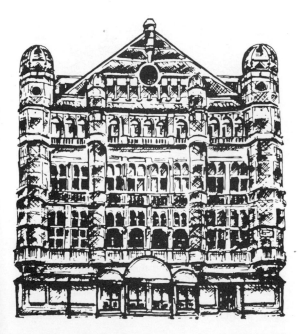

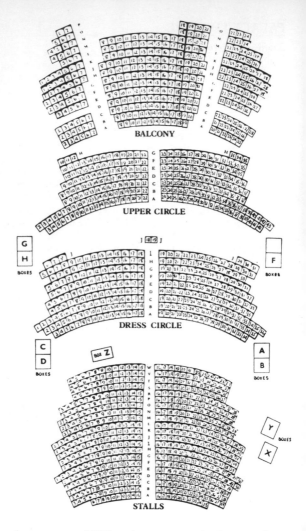

BALCONY

UPPER CIRCLE

DRESS CIRCLE

STALLS

began a run of 2385 performances, and a few years later *Jesus Christ Superstar* became on of the longest running-musicals of the time, playing the Palace for eight years.

The building itself was, meanwhile, becoming oddly neglected, with its façade partially dismantled and a strangely abandoned air about it. With Andrew Lloyd Webber's involvement and the formation of the Really Useful Theatre Company to raise money for refurbishment, it is hoped that the Palace will regain some of its former glory; some internal work has already been done, and (as we write) plans are afoot to restore the façade, currently hidden behind the giant neon display for (another huge success) *Les Misérables*.

BOOKING

£5-£18.50/concessions: only for Thursday matinées, for OAPs and students/telephone booking: pay within seven days of making reservation/postal booking: cheques to 'Palace Theatre', include SAE/credit cards: Visa-Barclaycard, Access-Mastercard, Diners' Club, American Express.

GETTING THERE

buses 1, 14, 19, 22, 24, 29, 38, 55, 176 to Cambridge Circus; theatre is on west side. 7, 8, 25, 73, 134 to Tottenham Court Road station; walk down Charing Cross Road, theatre on right. 3, 6, 11, 12, 13, 15, 23, 53, 77, 77A, 88, 159, 170, 172 to Trafalgar Square; walk uphill through St Martin's Place (National Gallery on left), bear left up west side of Charing Cross Road and continue to Cambridge Circus, theatre on left.

underground *Northern or Piccadilly Line* to Leicester Square; take Charing Cross Road exit, walk uphill to Cambridge Circus, theatre on left. *Central or Northern Line* to Tottenham Court Road; walk down Charing Cross Road to Cambridge Circus, theatre on right. *Bakerloo Line* to Piccadilly Circus; take Shaftesbury Avenue exit and walk up Shaftesbury Avenue to Cambridge Circus, theatre on left. *Jubilee Line* to Charing Cross Station; take Strand exit to Trafalgar Square, then continue as from buses to Trafalgar Square.

British Rail Trains to Charing Cross Station, then directions as from Charing Cross underground.

PALLADIUM – see LONDON PALLADIUM

PENTAMETERS THEATRE

The Three Horseshoes Pub, 28 Heath Street,
Hampstead NW3
Map refs: SF 46 D10, A-Z 44A1
Booking: 435 6757 (answerphone)

Fringe (plays)/flexible raked seating/open acting area/ capacity 100/view ***/audibility ***/a-c: none/heat: none/ wheelchair access/full pub facilities downstairs (no evening meals)/extras: poetry and play readings/ performances: 7.30pm & 9.30pm Tues-Sun/12.30am Fri-Sun.

Located upstairs over Hampstead's Three Horseshoes Pub, the Pentameters features a variety of lively, small productions ranging from alternative comedy to poetry readings and cabaret entertainment seven nights a week, with the emphasis on new works by new writers.

BOOKING

£1.50-£3.50/concessions: OAPs, students, unemployed/ telephone booking: collect-pay 15 minutes before performance/postal booking: cheques to 'Pentameters', include SAE or collect at door/credit cards: none.

GETTING THERE

buses 268 to Hampstead Station; walk uphill in Heath Street, look for Three Horseshoes Pub a few yards along.

underground *Northern Line* to Hampstead; right out of station and continue as for Hampstead buses.

British Rail South End Green; walk up South End Green and Pond Street, keeping hospital on left, to Rosslyn Hill Road, then catch a 268 bus to Hampstead underground station and proceed as for Hampstead buses. Alternatively, walk up Rosslyn Hill Road, Hampstead High Street to station and proceed as for Hampstead buses, (approx. 600 yards).

PHOENIX THEATRE

Charing Cross Road WC2H 0JP
Map refs: SF 140 G6, A-Z 60d 3D
Box Office: 836 2294 (10am-8pm Mon-Sat)
Credit card booking: 240 9661

Mainstream (plays, musicals)/traditional auditorium/ proscenium stage/capacity 1012/view***/audibility***/ a-c**/heat**/wheelchair access to dress circle, assistance to other seating sections, adapted rest rooms (notify management in advance)/snacks/five bars/performance times vary with production: see press.

The smart-looking little Phoenix theatre with its bright neo-classical façade and 30s modern entrance, has long been associated in memory with Noel Coward. Coward's *Private Lives*, with The Master, Gertrude Lawrence and Laurence Olivier heading the cast opened the theatre in 1930; and a number of Coward's later hits, notably *Tonight at 8.30* and *Quadrille* had their debuts here as well. In more recent years, true to its stylish beginings, the Phoenix has earned a reputation for mounting intelligent, provocative, often quite adventurous productions more familiarly associated with London's subsidized theatre sector than with the conventional and financially cautious West End. Mr. Coward's ghost has not yet been spotted at the foyer bar that was named after him in 1969, but his excellent spirit is quite obviously abroad somewhere in the building.

BOOKING

Concessions: OAPs, students, unemployed (contact box

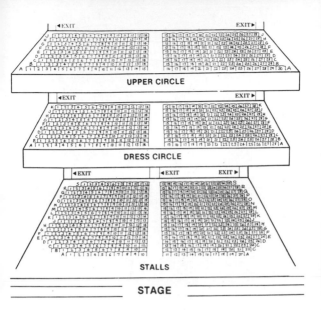

UPPER CIRCLE

DRESS CIRCLE

STALLS

STAGE

office for details)/telephone booking: pay within 4 working days of making reservation/postal booking: cheques to 'Phoenix Theatre', include SAE/credit cards: Visa-Barclaycard, Access-Mastercard, Diners' Club, American Express.

GETTING THERE

buses 1, 14, 19, 22, 24, 29, 38, 55, 176 to Cambridge Circus (or nearest in Charing Cross Road, walk uphill in Charing Cross to Foyles bookshop, theatre across street at Phoenix Passage. 7, 8, 25, 73, 134 to Tottenham Court Road Station (St. Giles Circus); walk downhill in Charing Cross Road approx. 300 yards, theatre on left.

underground *Central Line, Northern Line* to Tottenham Court Road; directions as for Tottenham Court Road buses.

PICCADILLY THEATRE

Denman Street W1V 8DY
Map refs: SF 140 D10, A-Z 60c C4
Box Office: 437 4506 (10am-8pm Mon-Sat)
Credit card booking: 379, 6565, 741 9999, 379 6433
Goup booking: 836 3962, 930 6123
Stage door: 437 2397

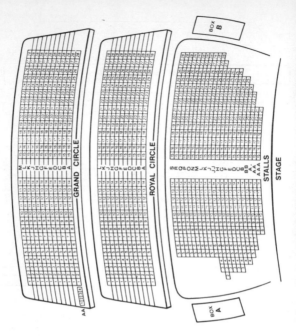

Mainstream (plays, musicals)/traditional auditorium proscenium stage/capacity 1170/view ***/audibility ***/a-c ***/heat ***/wheelchair access to one box, access to rest-rooms/snacks/three bars/performance times vary with production: see press.

Opened in 1928, the handsome but rather conservatively designed Piccadilly (it looks more like a bank than a theatre) has served largely as a home for musicals, classical revivals, and several Royal Shakespeare Company transfers. *Who's Afraid of Virginia Woolf?* had its first London run here, and *Educating Rita* ran nealy 2000 performances beginning in 1980.

BOOKING

Concessions: OAPs, students, under-24 British Rail card holders, unemployed, registered deaf or blind/telephone booking: pay within 7 days of making reservation/postal booking: cheques to 'Piccadilly Theatre', include SAE/ credit cards: Visa-Barclaycard, Access-Mastercard, Diners' Club, American Express.

GETTING THERE

buses 3, 6, 9, 12, 13, 14, 15, 19, 22, 23, 38, 53, 55, 88, 159 to Piccadilly Circus; to entrance of Shaftesbury Avenue, left into Denman Street just a few steps along, theatre on right at Sherwood Street. 1, 24, 29, 176 to Cambridge Circus;

walk down Shaftesbury Avenue, right into Denman Street, theatre on right. 11, 77, 77A, 170, 172 to Trafalgar Square; walk down Pall Mall East, right up Haymarket to Piccadilly Circus, continue as for Piccadilly Circus buses.

underground *Bakerloo Line, Piccadilly Line* to Piccadilly Circus; Shaftesbury Avenue exit, left into Denman Street, theatre on right.

British Rail Trains to Charing Cross Station; main exit, walk diagonally across Trafalgar Square to Pall Mall East, continue as for Trafalgar Square buses.

PLAYERS THEATRE

Villiers Street WC2N 6NQ
Map refs: SF 140 L12, A-Z 60d E4
Box Office: 839 1134 (10am-8pm closing Tues-Sun)
Membership details: 839 1676
Stage door: 839 5086

Mainstream (traditional Victorian-Edwardian music hall)/ open raked seating/proscenium thrust stage (apron stage)/capacity 260/view ***/audibility ***/a-c */heat **/ wheelchair access (notify management in advance), but rest-rooms difficult for disabled/one restaurant adjoining theatre (6.30pm-11.30pm, Sun 6.45; book in advance)/one sandwich-coffee bar in theatre (7pm-11pm Tues-Sat)/two bars/extras: dancing on stage after performance; smoking allowed/performances: 8.30pm Tues-Sat, 8pm Sun.

The Players Theatre Club, founded in 1929, occupied several buildings around the West End before finally taking up permanent residence, in 1945, in an old Victorian variety theatre called Gatti's Under-the-Arches Music Hall, beneath Hungerford railway bridge. Dedicated wholeheartedly to the joys of the Gay-90s, the Players continues to produce, as it always has, a new program of authentic Victorian music hall entertainment every fortnight.

BOOKING

Membership only/full membership: £17.50 annual subscription plus £12.50 entrance fee (first year); member may then come as often as desired; full membership for subsequent years £17.50 only/husband-wife full membership £30.00 annual subscription plus £20.00 entrance fee (first year)/temporary membership: 1 week £6.00, quarterly £12.00/each guest accompanying a member £5.00/concessions: students, nurses £3.00/ telephone bookings accepted (Sat-Sun from 5.30pm, postal booking: membership and booking by post accepted, cheques to 'Players Theatre', include SAE/credit cards: Visa-Barclaycard, Access-Mastercard.

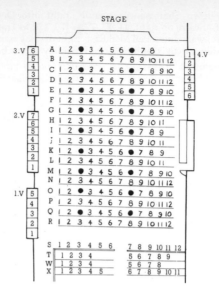

GETTING THERE

buses 1, 6, 9, 11, 13, 15, 23, 77, 77A, 172, 176 to Charing Cross Station (or nearest stop in Strand to Villiers Street, Villiers Street commences at Strand, just left of Charing Cross Station as you face the main entrance. Walk down Villiers Street to railway bridge, theatre built under bridge arches—can't miss it! 3, 12, 24, 29, 53, 88, 159 to Trafalgar Square; to Charing Cross Station and continue as for Charing Cross Station buses. 4, 5, 68, 171, 188, 501, 502, 513 to Aldwych; walk west to Strand, along Strand to Charing Cross Station, continue as for Charing Cross Station buses.

underground *District or Circle Line* to Embankment; Villiers Street exit, theatre within sight. *Bakerloo Line, Jubilee Line, Northern Line* to Charing Cross Station; Villiers Street exit, continue as for Charing Cross buses.

British Rail Trains to Charing Cross Station, directions as for Charing Cross underground.

PLAYHOUSE THEATRE

Northumberland Avenue, WC2
Re-opening summer 1987 after a long stint as a BBC radio studio, the Playhouse was known in its hey day as 'the home of comedy'. Alec Guinness made his stage début here in 1934. Call 01-240 8415 for current information.

PRINCE EDWARD THEATRE

Old Compton Street, W1V 6HS
Map refs: SF 140 17G, A-Z 60d D3
Box Office: 434 8951 (10am-8pm Mon-Sat)
Credit card booking: 836 3464 (24-hr, 7 days per week)
Stage door: 439 3041

Mainstream (plays, musicals)/traditional auditorium proscenium stage/capacity 1672/viewing ***/audibility ***/ a-c **/heat **/two wheelchair spaces in Royal Box/four bars/performances: 7.30pm Mon-Sat + 2.30pm Thurs and Sat.

The large, rather stolid-looking Prince Edward was the first of several London theatres to be built in the 1930s, their designs either insistently modern or rather stuffily neo-classical (the Prince Edward being decidedly one of the latter group). Early misfortune with musical and revue entertainments caused the Prince Edward to be transformed into a cabaret-restaurant called the London Casino in 1950, and later into the West End home of Cinerama. A blend of film and stage entertainment followed in the 1960s and 70s, and the theatre looked set to continue its precarious course almost indefinitely…Then in 1978 the musical *Evita* arrived, which ran until 1986, to be followed by *Chess*, playing to full houses as we write.

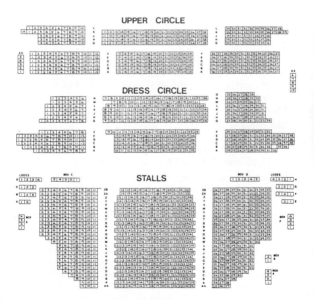

BOOKING

£8-£20/concessions: none/postal booking: cheques to 'Prince Edward Theatre', with SAE/credit cards: Visa-Barclaycard, Access-Mastercard, American Express.

GETTING THERE

buses 1, 14, 19, 22, 24, 29, 38, 55, 176 to Cambridge Circus; walk uphill along Charing Cross Road for Approx. 50 yards, then turn left into Old Compton Street, theatre on right a few yards along. 7, 8, 25, 73, 134 to Tottenham Court Road Station; walk down Charing Cross Road for approx 400 yards, turn right into Old Compton Street, theatre on right a few yards along. 3, 6, 9, 12, 13, 14, 15, 23, 53, 176 to Piccadilly Circus; walk up Shaftesbury Avenue to Cambridge Circus and proceed as for Cambridge Circus buses.

underground *Northern or Piccadilly Line* to Leicester Square; walk up Charing Cross Road, around Cambridge Circus, then another 50 yards and turn left into Old Compton Street, theatre on right a few yards along. *Central or Northern Line* to Tottenham Court Road; proceed as for Tottenham Court Road buses.

The Prince Edward, incidentally, is the theatre the baffled American couple in the Introduction were looking for.

PRINCE OF WALES THEATRE

Coventry Street W1V 8AS
Map refs: SF 140 E10, A-Z 60d D4
Box Office: 930 8681, 930 8682 (10am-8pm Mon-Sat)
Credit card booking: 930 0844, 930 0845, 930 0846, 741 9999
Goup booking: 930 6123
Stage door: 930 1432

Mainstream (musicals, plays)/traditional auditorium/proscenium stage/capacity 1123/view ***/audibility ***/a-c ***/heat ***/disabled facilities: none/snacks/three bars/performances: 7.30pm Mon-Sat, 3pm Thurs & Sat.

Opened originally as the Prince's Theatre in 1884, renamed 2 years later, and completely rebuilt in 1936, the present Prince of Wales looks as much like a furniture warehouse as the Piccadilly does a bank and the Prince Edward a public library. Appearances notwithstanding, the theatre is extremely comfortable inside and has had a consistently cheerful history as a West End home for gloriously lavish revues and wonderfully popular musicals like *Funny Girl*, *Sweet Charity*, and *The World of Susie Wong*.

BOOKING

£6.50-£15.50/concessions: OAPs, students, (variable

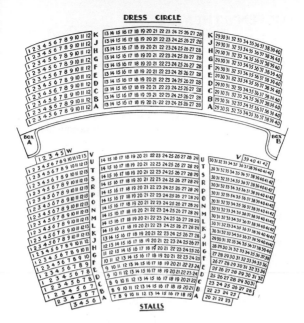

DRESS CIRCLE

STALLS

details, contact box office), groups of 15 or more/telephone booking: pay within four days of making reservation/ postal booking: cheques to 'Prince of Wales Theatre', include SAE/credit cards: Visa-Barclaycard, Access-Mastercard, American Express.

GETTING THERE

buses 3, 6, 9, 12, 13, 14, 15, 19, 22, 23, 38, 53, 55, 88, 159 to Piccadilly Circus; from Piccadilly, walk straight ahead into Coventry Street, theatre a few yards along on right. 1, 24, 29, 176 to Leicester Square; Cranbourn Street to Leicester Square, continue straight ahead through Square into Coventry Street, theatre on left. 11, 77, 77A, 170, 172 to Trafalgar Square; walk up St. Martin's Street (keeping National Gallery on your right), past Leicester Square, left into New Coventry Street and on into Coventry Street, theatre on left.

underground *Bakerloo Line, Piccadilly Line* to Piccadilly Circus; Haymarket exit, right into Coventry Street, theatre a few yards along on right. *Northern Line* to Leicester Square; Charing Cross West exit and continue as for Leicester Square buses.

British Rail Trains to Charing Cross Station, to Trafalgar Square and continue as for Trafalgar Square buses.

QUEEN'S THEATRE

Shaftesbury Avenue W1V 8BA
Map refs: SF 140 E-F9, A-Z 60d D3
Box Office: 734 1166, 734 1167 (10am-8pm Mon-Sat)
Credit card booking: 734 0261, 734 0120
Stage door: 734 1348

Mainstream (plays)/traditional auditorium/proscenium stage/capacity 979/view ***/audibility ***/a-c */heat ***/ three bars/performance times vary with production: see press.

Built in 1908 by W.G.R. Sprague as a companion building to the Globe, the Queen's Theatre is the easternmost of the four theatres grouped along the north side of Shaftesbury Avenue below Cambridge Circus. Unfortunately, exterior renovations due to war damage were only begun in the late 1950s, a period of British architecture now notorious for its dreadful (though nobly motivated) experiments in 'social engineering'. If not for its marquee and a sign reading 'Queens Theatre', the once graceful neo-classical building would be all but indistinguishable from dozens of 1950s council tenements that are presently being demolished around London because nobody wants to live in them. Sprague's finely proportioned Edwardian interior has largely survived, however, and so has the theatre's long-standing reputation for the staging of top-flight comedies and dramas.

BOOKING

telephone booking: pay within three days of making reservation/postal booking: cheques to 'Queens Theatre', include SAE/credit cards: Visa-Barclaycard, Access-Mastercard, American Express.

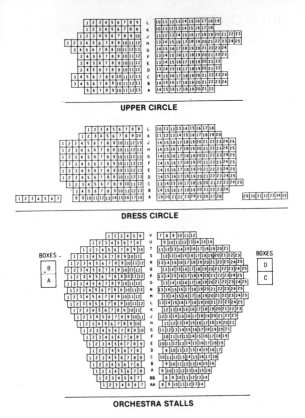

UPPER CIRCLE

DRESS CIRCLE

BOXES

B

A

BOXES

D

C

ORCHESTRA STALLS

STAGE

GETTING THERE

buses 1, 14, 19, 22, 24, 29, 38, 55, 176 to Cambridge Circus (or nearest stop in Shaftesbury Avenue to Wardour Street); from all stops, look for theatre at the east (uphill) end of the group of four theatres on the north side of Shaftesbury Avenue approx. half way between Cambridge Circus and Piccadilly Circus. 3, 6, 9, 12, 13, 15, 23, 53, 88, 159 to Piccadilly Circus; to Shaftesbury Avenue and continue as for Cambridge Circus buses.

underground *Bakerloo Line, Piccadilly Line* to Piccadilly Circus; Shaftesbury Avenue exit and continue as for Cambridge Circus buses. *Northern Line* to Leicester Square; Cranbourn Street to Leicester Square, walk through square, right in Wardour Street to Shaftesbury Avenue, theatre almost directly across street.

QUESTORS THEATRE

Mattock Lane, Ealing W5 5BQ
Map refs: SF 72 E2, A-Z 56 A2
Box Office: 567 5184 (6.45pm-8pm Mon-Sun)
Membership: 567 8736

Fringe (amateur/professional—plays, musicals)/arena seating/open platform stage/capacity 325-450/view ***/audibility ***/a-c ***/heat ***/some disabled seating (notify management in advance, performances: 7.45pm Mon-Sun.

A smallish, handsomely designed theatre club serving suburban Ealing, the Questors features both amateur and professional touring productions of new and

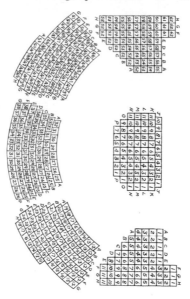

experimental works as well as mainstream comedy, drama and musicals.

BOOKING

£1.50-£3.00/concessions: members, otherwise contact box office/telephone booking: details from box office/postal booking: cheques to 'Questors Theatre', include SAE/credit cards: none.

GETTING THERE

buses 65, 83, 207, 274, E1, E2 to Uxbridge Road (town hall) or nearest stop to Bond Street; Bond Street to Mattock Lane, sharp right, theatre just around corner on left. 112, 273 to Ealing Broadway; walk down The Broadway, right into Uxbridge Road, left into Bond Street, sharp right into Mattock Lane, theatre just around corner on left.

underground *Central Line*, *District Line* to Ealing Broadway; directions as for Ealing Broadway buses.

British Rail Trains to Ealing Broadway; directions as for Ealing Broadway buses. To West Ealing; right out of station into Argyle Road, left into Uxbridge Road, right into Culmington Road, left into Mattock Lane, theatre on right approx. 800 yards.

RICHMOND THEATRE

The Green, Richmond, Surrey TW9 1QJ
Map refs: SF 84 G12, A-Z 72 B4
Box Office: 940 0088 (10am-8pm Mon-Sat)
Stage door: 940 5959

Mainstream (plays, musicals)/traditional auditorium/ proscenium stage/capacity 920/view ***/audibility ***/a-c: none/heat ***/wheelchair spectators must be helped into seats, hearing loops, adapted rest rooms (notify management in advance)/snacks/one wine bar/four bars/ performances: 7.45pm Mon-Fri, 2.30pm Wed, 5pm & 8.15pm Sat.

Opened in 1899, and the most perfectly preserved of all Frank Matcham's London theatres, the Richmond

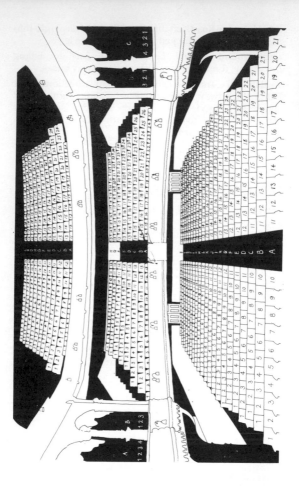

features a red brick and terracotta Baroque facade flanked prominently by two splendid, cupola-topped towers in brick and stone. The only architectural anomaly—thank goodness not a permanent one—is a large, white, twin-peaked circus tent-marquee which was erected over the entrance in the 1950s (in misguided homage to Raquel Welch, perhaps), and which, to quote historian John Earl again, '...should be removed to the accompaniment of dancing in the streets'. Throughout most of its history the Richmond has mounted revivals of popular comedies and dramas, and has also been regularly employed as a try-out theatre for future West End productions. Now under new management, the Theatre also puts on regular Sunday night concerts, including jazz, classical music, rock, poetry recitals etc.

BOOKING

£2.50-£8.00/concessions: OAPs, children, groups of 10 or more/telephone booking: pay within three working days of making reservation/postal booking: cheques to 'Richmond Theatre Ltd', include SAE/credit cards: Visa-Barclaycard, Access-Mastercard.

GETTING THERE

buses 7, 27, 33, 37, 65, 71, 90B, 202, 270, 290 to Richmond Town Centre; from town centre, take either Hill Street or George Street to King Street, right into Greenside, left into The Green, theatre visible a few yards along.

underground *District Line* to Richmond Station; left out of station down The Quadrant, right into Duke Street, left into Greenside, ½ right into The Green, theatre visible a few yards along.

British Rail Trains to Richmond Station; directions as for Richmond underground.

RIVERSIDE STUDIOS

Crisp Road, Hammersmith W6 9RL
Map refs: SF 144 C11, A-Z 74 C1
Box Office: 748 3354 (10am-9pm Tues-Sun)
Credit card booking: 379 6433 (Ticketmaster)

Fringe (plays, dance)/flexible raked seating/open platform stage (adaptable to proscenium productions)/capacity 400/ view ***/audibility ***/a-c **/heat **/wheelchair access/ one restaurant, 10am-11pm/one bar/extra-art gallery, exhibitions, theatrical workshops, musical events, children's shows, dance classes/performances: 8pm seven days per week.

Originally a film studio in the 1940s, then a BBC-TV studio, Riverside Studios has been fighting courageous financial battles for much of its 10-year existence, a most unjust circumstance considering the fine fringe productions that have been staged here in the past decade, and the excellent and varied workshop programmes that are conducted for writers, choreographers, theatre designers and independent film makers. One of London's most important and worthwhile multi-purpose arts centres and a vital force for the ongoing health of the English fringe theatre movement.

BOOKING

£2.50-£6.00/concessions: OAPs,students, unemployed and Equity members/telephone booking: collect-pay before performance/postal booking: cheques to 'Riverside Trust' include SAE or collect at box office/credit cards: (only through Ticketmaster) Visa-Barclaycard, Access-Mastercard, Diners' Club, American Express.

GETTING THERE

buses 9, 33, 72, 710, 714, 715 to Hammersmith Bridge Road (nearest stop to Hammersmith Bridge); from Hammersmith Bridge walk east in Lower Mall (with river on right), left into Queen Caroline, right into Crisp Road, look for Riverside Studios a few yards along. 11, 220, 283, 295 to Fulham Palace Road (nearest stop to Chancellor's Road; walk down Chancellor's Road, right into Crisp Road, look for Riverside Studios a few yards along. 11, 27, 73, 91, 260, 266, 267, 290, 295, 701, 704, 730, 740, X12 to Hammersmith Broadway: walk south in Fulham Palace Road, under Hammersmith flyover, right into Queen Caroline, left into Crisp Road, look for Riverside Studios a few yards along.

underground *District Line, Piccadilly Line* to Hammersmith; directions as for Hammersmith Broadway buses.

ROYAL COURT THEATRE

Sloane Square, Chelsea SW1 8AS
Map refs: SF 147 R7, A-Z 76 C1-(top of page)
Box Office: 730 1745 main theatre, 730 2554 upstairs studio
(10am-8pm Mon-Sat)
Credit card booking: 730 1745
Stage door: 730 5174

Main Theatre Fringe (plays)/traditional auditorium/proscenium stage/capacity 401/view ** (some restricted seats – sold last)/audibility ***/a-c */heat **/wheelchair access/ adapted rest-rooms/performances: 8pm Mon-Sat.

Theatre Upstairs Fringe (plays, performance) / flexible seating / open acting area / capacity 100/view *** /audibility*** / a-c* / heat** / disabled facilities: none **Both theatres:** one coffee bar/two bars/bookshop/performances: 7.30pm Mon-Sat.

Probably the most important and influential of London's fringe theatres today, the Royal Court opened in its present red brick and stone Italianate building in 1888 with a series of successful comedies, notably by Pinero, and then in 1904, under Harley Granville-Barker's management, turned to the classical revivals and *avant-garde* works by Shaw, Galsworthy and their contemporaries that quickly established the theatre, along

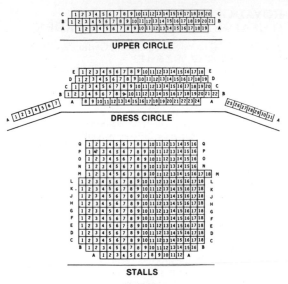

UPPER CIRCLE

DRESS CIRCLE

STALLS

STAGE

with the Old Vic, as a principal centre of serious new theatre in 20th-century England. The Court was forced to close during the Depression, and interior bomb damage during World War II forced it to remain closed until funds were found for rebuilding in 1952. But in 1956 the theatre began its second great period under George Devine (see history), and though in recent years times have been difficult financially, the Court has still managed to remain a central driving force in contemporary English theatre; an invaluable first venue for new and experimental works of all kinds, and a 'home' where new directors, actors, designers, and particularly playwrights are actively encouraged to show the world what they can do.

BOOKING

£3.00-£12.50/concessions: OAPs, students, unemployed/ telephone booking: pay within three working days of making reservation/postal booking: cheques to 'Royal Court Theatre', include SAE/credit cards: Visa-Barclaycard, Access-Mastercard, American Express, (credit card phone booking stops at 7pm).

GETTING THERE

buses 11, 19, 22, 137 to Sloane Square (or nearest stop); theatre on south side of Sloane Square, just beside underground station.

underground *District or Circle Line* to Sloane Square; theatre next to station.

ROYAL OPERA HOUSE
(THEATRE ROYAL, COVENT GARDEN)

Bow Street and Floral Street, Covent Garden WC2E 7QA
Map refs: SF 140 L7, A-Z 60d E3
Box Office: 240 1066, 240 1911 (10am-8pm Mon-Sat)
Credit card booking: 240 1066, 240 1911
Information (24-hour): 240 9815, 836 6903
Stage door: 240 1200

Mainstream (opera, ballet)/traditional auditorium/proscenium stage/capacity 2107/view (centre sections) *** (side sections) **/audibility ***/a-c: none/heat *** (very warm at top of auditorium)/wheelchair access to some sections (notify management in advance)/one buffet-restaurant (Crush Bar)/cold meals served to boxes (tel. 836 9453 for reservations)/six bars with cold buffet/performances: 7.30pm Mon-Sat, 2.30pm Tues.

One of London's oldest and most distinguished theatres, the present Covent Garden has been, since its re-christening as the Royal Opera House in 1939, London's principal venue for the production of traditional opera and ballet. Three theatres have stood on the famous Covent Garden site since the first was built in 1732, the present one being a monument of neo-classical grandeur designed by Sir Edward Barry in 1858. (See London theatre history for details).

BOOKING

£4.00-£37.00/concessions: contact box office/telephone

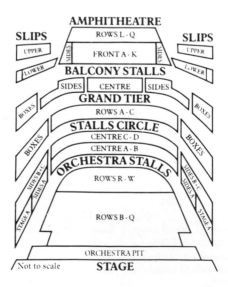

booking: pay within three working days of making reservation/postal booking: cheques to 'Royal Opera House,' include SAE, address to: Royal Opera House, 48 Floral Street, London WC2E 7QA/subscription booking and mailing list details: contact box office/credit cards: Visa-Barclaycard, Access-Mastercard, Diners' Club.

GETTING THERE

buses   1, 4, 5, 6, 9, 11, 13, 15, 23, 68, 77, 77A, 170, 171, 172, 176, 188, 501, 502, 513 to west end of Aldwych, walk up Wellington Street approx. 400 yards, theatre on left at corner of Floral Street.

underground   *Piccadilly Line* to Covent Garden; right out of station, right around corner into James Street, left into Floral Street, theatre on left at corner of Bow Street. *Northern Line* to Leicester Square; from any exit take Cranbourn Street to Long Acre, continue on past Covent Garden underground, right into James Street, left into Floral Street, theatre on left at corner of Bow Street.

British Rail   Trains to Charing Cross Station; Strand exit, right in Strand approx. 500 yards, left up Wellington Street, theatre on left approx. 400 yards along at corner of Floral Street.

ROYAL SHAKESPEARE – see BARBICAN CENTRE.

SADLER'S WELLS THEATRE

Rosebery Avenue EC1R 4TN
Map refs: SF 133 V12, A-Z 46 A4
Box Office: 278 8916 (10.30am-7.30pm),
278 5450 (information)
Credit card booking: 278 8916
Group bookiing: 278 6853
Stage Door: 278 6563

Mainstream (opera, ballet, dance)/traditional auditorium/ proscenium stage/capacity 1499/view ***/audibility ***/ a-c */heat ***/wheelchair access/hearing loops/one buffet-restaurant (tel. 278 6763 before 4pm to book)/three bars/ performances: 7.30pm Mon-Sat, 2.30pm Sat (some variations).

The first theatre on the Sadler's Wells site opened in 1683 as a music hall. The present theatre, a 30s-Modernist building with neo-classical allusions, was built for Lilian Baylis and opened in 1931 as a proposed North London companion to the Old Vic. The scheme failed, however, (though through no lack of energy on Miss Baylis's part), and from 1934 onwards Shakespeare was replaced by ballet and opera. The theatre was for many years the home of the English National Opera Company, (which moved to

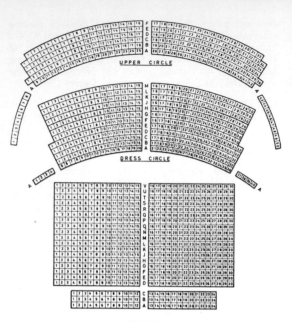

UPPER CIRCLE

DRESS CIRCLE

STALLS

the London Coliseum in 1968), and is still home for both the Sadler's Wells Ballet Company and the New Sadler's Wells Opera Company, as well as providing a showcase for the best British and international dance, ballet and opera companies.

BOOKING

£2.50-£15.00/concessions: OAPs, students, unemployed, (contact box office for details)/telephone booking: pay within four working days of making reservation/postal booking: cheques to 'Sadler's Wells Trust Ltd.', include SAE/credit cards: Visa-Barclaycard, Access-Mastercard, Diners' Club, American Express.

GETTING THERE

buses 19, 38, 171, 279 to Sadler's Wells; bus stops just outside theatre. 4, 30, 43, 73, 104, 277, 279A to Angel; walk down St. John Street to intersection with Rosebery Avenue, theatre on right.

underground *Northern Line* to Angel; directions as for Angel buses (5-minute walk).

ST MARTIN'S THEATRE

West Street, WC2H 9NH
Map refs: SF 140 8H, A-Z 60d D3
Box Office: 836 1443 (10am-8pm Mon-Sat)
Credit card booking: 379 6433
Stage door. 836 1086

Mainstream (plays)/traditional auditorium/proscenium stage/capacity 550/view ***/audibility ***/a-c ***/heat ***/ disabled facilities: contact Box Office/three bars/ performances: 8pm Mon-Sat + 2.45pm Tues, 5pm Sat.

Designed by W.G.R. Sprague as a companion building to the Ambassadors Theatre, but not built until 1916—three years after the Ambassadors—the St Martin's features a strong, forthright, classical façade with an equally strong, almost severely classical interior. The theatre played mostly serious works by new English playwrights until the mid-1940s, and then went over to a mixed policy of comedy, revue, thrillers and lighter drama. Anthony Shaffer's extremely successful *Sleuth* began a long run here in 1970, and in 1974 history's longest-running play, *The Mousetrap*, transferred from the Ambassadors next door, and is *still* playing.

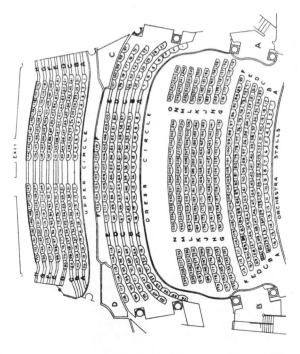

BOOKING

£3.50-£9.50/no concessions/postal booking: cheques to 'St Martin's Theatre' with SAE/credit cards: Visa-Barclaycard, Access-Mastercard, Diners' Club, American Express.

GETTING THERE

buses 1, 14, 19, 22, 24, 38, 55, 176 to Cambridge Circus; from east side walk a few steps into Tower Street, then turn right into West Street and left around the corner, theatre on left just past Ambassadors a few yards along. 7, 8, 25, 73, 134 to Tottenham Court Road Station; walk down east side of Charing Cross Road to Cambridge Circus, then proceed as above. 3, 6, 11, 12, 13, 15, 23, 53, 77, 77A, 88, 159, 170, 172 to Trafalgar Square; walk uphill through St Martin's Place (National Gallery on left), and on up east side of Charing Cross Road to Cambridge Circus, then as above.

underground *Northern or Piccadilly Line* to Leicester Square; take Charing Cross Road East exit, walk up to Cambridge Circus, then as above. *Central or Northern Line* to Tottenham Court Road; walk down east side of Charing Cross Road to Cambridge Circus, then as above. *Bakerloo or Piccadilly Line* to Piccadilly Circus; take Shaftesbury Avenue exit, walk up Shaftesbury Avenue to Cambridge Circus, then as above. *Jubilee Line* to Charing Cross Station; take Strand exit to Trafalgar Square, and proceed as for Trafalgar Square buses.

British Rail Trains to Charing Cross Station; directions as from underground station.

SAVOY THEATRE

Savoy Court, Strand WC2R 0ET
Map refs: SF 140 M10, A-Z 60d F4
Box Office: 836 8888 (10am-8pm Mon-Sat)
Credit card booking: 836 0479, 379 6219
Stage door: 836 8117

Mainstream (plays)/traditional auditorium/proscenium stage/capacity 1122/view ***/audibility ***/a-c */heat ***/ wheelchair access (notify management in advance)/four bars/performance: times vary with production: see press.

Built in 1881 for Richard D'Oyly Carte as a home for Gilbert and Sullivan operettas, the Savoy enjoyed continual success with musical comedies until 1907, when Harley Granville-Barker moved from the Royal Court and began staging more serious works, notably new plays by Shaw, but also many fine Shakespeare revivals. After renovation in 1929, the theatre became a home for popular comedies, musicals and light drama; a policy which has continued to the present day. Architecturally, the theatre is renowned

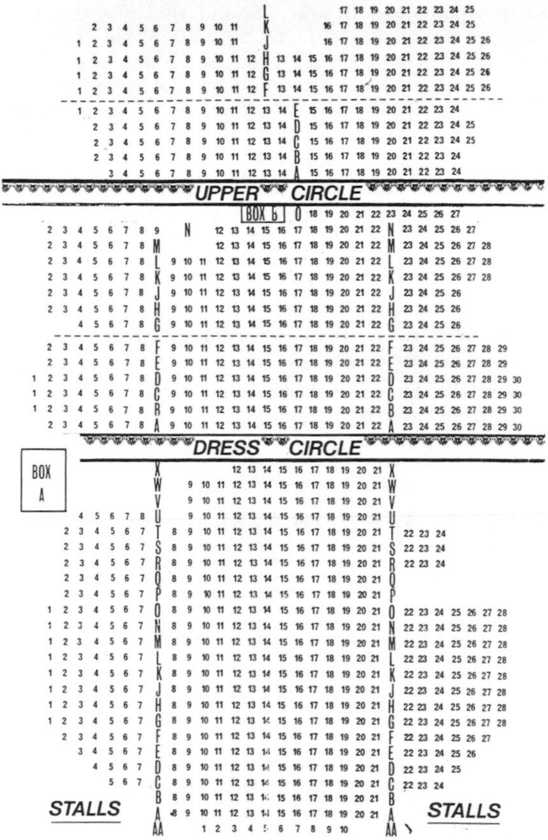

UPPER CIRCLE

BOX 6

DRESS CIRCLE

BOX A

STALLS   STALLS

for its striking and almost perfectly preserved Art Deco interior.

BOOKING

Concessions: students (matinee only)/telephone booking: pay within three days of making reservation/postal booking: cheques to 'Savoy Theatre', include SAE/credit cards: Visa-Barclaycard, Access-Mastercard, Diners' Club, American Express.

GETTING THERE

buses 1, 6, 9, 11, 13, 15, 23, 77, 77A, 170, 172, 176 to Strand (nearest stop to Southampton Street); look for the

Savoy Hotel on south side of Strand, theatre entrance in hotel courtyard. 4, 5, 171, 188, 501, 502, 513 to Aldwych; walk along Strand toward Trafalgar Square approx. 200 yards, theatre entry on left in courtyard of Savoy Hotel. 3, 12, 24, 29, 53, 88, 159 to Trafalgar Square; walk approx. 600 yards along Strand, theatre entrance on right in Savoy Hotel courtyard.

underground *Piccadilly Line* to Aldwych (Aldwych direction); Strand exit, continue as for Aldwych buses. *Bakerloo Line, Jubilee Line or Northern Line* to Charing Cross Station; Strand exit, turn right into Strand and continue as for Trafalgar Square buses. *District or Circle Line* to Embankment; Villiers Street exit, walk up Villiers Street (away from river), right into Strand, continue as for Trafalgar Square buses.

British Rail Trains to Charing Cross Station; directions as for Charing Cross underground.

SHAFTESBURY THEATRE OF COMEDY

Shaftesbury Avenue WC2H 8DP
Map refs: SF 140 J5, A-Z 60d E2
Box Office: 379 5399 (10am-8pm Mon-Sat)
Credit card booking: 741 9999
Group booking: 930 6123, 379 6433
Stage door: 836 8181

Mainstream (plays)/traditional auditorium/proscenium stage/capacity 1370/view ***/audibility ***/a-c */heat **/ wheelchair access (notify management in advance)/ snacks/five bars/performances: 8pm Mon-Fri, 3pm Wed, 5.30pm & 8.30pm Sat.

Notable architecturally for a not un-handsome neo-Georgian tower standing above characterless, hoarding-like walls, the history of the present Shaftesbury Theatre has been as uncertain as its exterior appearance. The original, opened in 1888, had consistent success with melodrama and musical comedy. But the second and present Shaftesbury, opened in 1911 as the Prince's Theatre, (it was re-christened in 1963), wandered from drama to ballet to pantomime to opera with only rare successes and no fixed policy until the American musical *Hair* opened in 1968. The show ran for 1997 performances; but even that triumph proved a mixed blessing, for just as the Shaftesbury was about to celebrate the big 2000 its ceiling collapsed, (vibrations, no doubt), and everything – theatre and show alike – had to be closed. Saved from demolition by the joint efforts of Alec Guinness and Paul Schofield, the building is now protected, (it does boast a wonderfully theatrical, neo-classical interior), but its

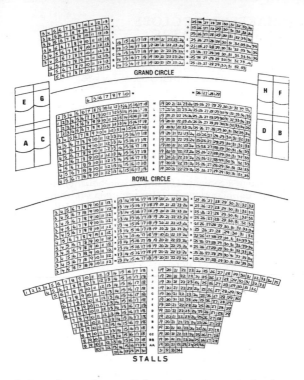

GRAND CIRCLE

ROYAL CIRCLE

STALLS

fortunes have only recently begun to revive again thanks, fittingly, to a resurgence in the popularity of farces.

BOOKING

£6.50-£12.50/concessions: contact box office/telephone booking: pay within three days of making reservation/ postal booking cheques to 'Shaftesbury Theatre of Comedy,' include SAE/credit cards: Visa-Barclaycard, Access-Mastercard, Diners' Club, American Express.

GETTING THERE

buses 5, 7, 8, 19, 22, 25, 35, 55, 68, 77A, 172, 188, 501 to Holborn Station; walk west down High Holborn (to your right as you face Kingsway), cross Drury Lane and look for theatre on right as you approach intersection with Shaftesbury Avenue. 1, 14, 24, 29, 38, 73, 134, 176 to Tottenham Court Road Station; St. Giles High Street to Shaftesbury Avenue, theatre across intersection at High Holborn.

underground *Central Line, Piccadilly Line* to Holborn; Kingsway exit and continue as for Holborn buses. *Central Line, Northern Line* to Tottenham Court Road; directions as for Tottenham Court Road buses.

SHAKESPEARE GLOBE
MUSEUM THEATRE

1 Bear Gardens, Bankside, Southwark SE1 9EB
Map refs: SF 142 A11, A-Z 61b D4
Box Office: 928 6342 (10am-5.30pm Tues-Sat,
2pm-6pm Sun)

Classical Elizabethan (plays, interludes, sketches)/
Elizabethan playhouse seating/Elizabethan platform
stage/capacity 90-100 (no seating in upper galleries)/
view ***/audibility ***/a-c ***/heat ***/extras: all facilities
and services of the museum/performances: 7.30pm Tues-
Sat, 6pm Sun.

Located in a converted Georgian warehouse on the site of
Elizabethan London's bear baiting arena, and only a short
distance from the site of Shakespeare's and Burbage's
original Globe Theatre, the theatre stages regular
performances of 16th and early 17th Century plays in
conjunction with the Museum's exhibitions of
Elizabethan theatre memorabilia. The stage is an
authentic replica of the Cockpit Theatre stage built in 1616.
The museum houses models and plans for the
reconstruction of the Globe Theatre.

BOOKING

£3.50/concessions: contact box office/no advance booking/
no credit cards.

GETTING THERE

buses 19, 44, 70, 95, 149, 184 to Southwark Bridge Road
(nearest stop to Park Street); facing bridge and river, walk
left in Park Street a few yards, right into Bear Gardens,
museum visible. 6, 9, 11, 15, 23, 76, 513 to Mansion House;
walk across Southwark Bridge to south bank, right into
Park Street, continue as for Southwark Bridge Road buses.

underground *District or Circle Line* to Mansion House;
directions as for Mansion House buses.

British Rail Trains to Cannon Street Station; to
Southwark Bridge and continue as for Mansion House
buses.

SOHO POLY

16 Riding House Street W1P 7PD
Map refs: SF 140 A2-3, A-Z 60c B2
Box Office: 636 9050 (2pm-8pm staff/other hours
answerphone

Fringe (plays)/flexible raked seating/open acting area/
capacity 50-60/view ***/audibility ***/a-c: none/heat **/

wheelchair access with assistance (notify management in advance)/snack bar (no alcohol)/performances: 8pm Mon-Sat.

Founded in a Soho basement in 1972, the Soho Poly has for more than a decade been one of London's most active and popular smaller fringe theatres, featuring new works not previously seen in London presented both by its own resident playing company and by visiting groups. New writing is strongly encouraged and in recent years the Poly has staged début works by Sue Townsend, Pam Gems, Howard Brenton and Barrie Keefe. John Hurt, Simon Callow, David Warner, Dianna Quick and Prunella Scales have all played the Poly in their time, and despite not having a license to serve alchohol, the theatre is a great favourite with actors.

BOOKING

£3.50-£2.75 / concessions: contact box office / telephone booking: pay within three days of making reservation/ postal booking: cheques to 'Soho Poly Theatre', include SAE or collect at door/credit cards: none.

GETTING THERE

buses 1, 3, 6, 7, 8, 12, 13, 15, 16A, 23, 25, 53, 73, 88, 113, 137, 159, 500 to Oxford Circus; find Great Portland Street (Peter Robinson department store stands on the north side of Oxford Street between Regent Street and Great Portland Street), walk up Great Portland Street approx. 350 yards, right into Riding House Street, theatre entry on right a few yards along (it's a basement, so keep your eyes peeled).

underground *Bakerloo Line, Central Line, Victoria Line* to Oxford Circus; Oxford Street north exit and continue as for Oxford Circus buses.

STRAND THEATRE

Aldwych WC2B 5LD
Map refs: SF 140 N8, A-Z 60d F3
Box Office: 836 2660, 836 4143, 836 5190 (10am-8pm
Mon-Sat)
Stage door: 836 4144

Mainstream (plays)/traditional auditorium/proscenium
stage/capacity 937/view ***/audibility ***/a-c **/heat ***/
wheelchair access (notify management in advance)/
snacks/four bars/performances: 8pm Mon-Fri, 2.30pm
Wed, 5.30pm & 8.30pm Sat.

Built by W.G.R. Sprague in 1905 as a companion building
to the Aldwych Theatre, (the 2 theatre's flank Sprague's
Waldorf Hotel), the Strand's elaborately neo-classical
facade and well-preserved Louis XVI interior combine to
create a particularly inviting atmosphere for a theatre
which has consistently housed successful comedy and
light drama from the year of its opening. Called the
Waldorf Theatre until 1911, the Strand is perhaps best
remembered as the original home of one of history's most
popular and finely written thrillers, *Arsenic and Old Lace*.

BOOKING

£5.00-£10.50/concessions: contact box office/telephone
booking: pay within 3 days of making reservation/postal
booking: cheques to 'Strand Theatre', include SAE/credit
cards: Visa-Barclaycard, Access-Mastercard, American
Express.

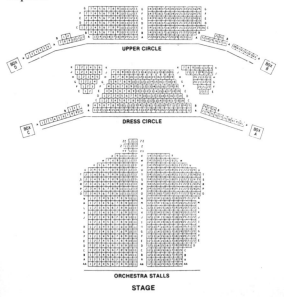

buses   1, 4, 5, 6, 9, 11, 13, 15, 23, 68, 77, 77A, 170, 171, 172, 188, 501 to Aldwych; theatre at west end of Aldwych near intersection of Catherine Street.

underground   *Piccadilly Line* to Aldwych; (Aldwych direction) directions as for Aldwych buses.

British Rail   Trains to Charing Cross Station; Strand exit, right along Strand approx. 500 yards, ½ left into Aldwych, theatre on left a few yards along.

THEATRE ROYAL, DRURY LANE

Catherine Street WC2E 7QA
Map refs: SF 140 M7, A-Z 60d F3
Box Office: 836 8108, 240 9066, 240 9067 (10am-8pm Mon-Sat)
Stage door: 836 3352

Mainstream (musicals)/traditional auditorium/proscenium stage/capacity 2283/view ** (some restricted seats in upper circle)/audibility ***/a-c */heat ***/wheelchair access (notify management in advance)/seven bars/performance times vary with production: see press.

The present Drury Lane, the fourth theatre on the site, was opened in 1812 and thus ranks as the oldest London theatre still in use. It is also one of only two active London theatres housed in a true—as opposed to a neo—Georgian building; (even its portico, added in 1820, is legitimately Georgian). The auditorium, however, was completely remodelled in 1920, and is now decorated in Empire style; a fine example of period renovation. For nearly three centuries the home of the greatest drama produced in English, the Drury Lane has, since the 1950s, been used principally for the staging of lavish musicals.

BOOKING

Telephone: pay within three days of making reservation/ postal booking: cheques to 'Theatre Royal Drury Lane ', include SAE/credit cards: Visa-Barclaycard, Access-Mastercard, American Express.

GETTING THERE

buses   1, 4, 5, 6, 9, 11, 13, 15, 23, 68, 77, 77A, 170, 171, 172, 188, 501 to Aldwych; from west end of Aldwych walk 2 blocks up Catherine Street, theatre on right at corner of Russell Street.

underground   *Piccadilly Line* to Aldwych; (Aldwych direction) directions as for Aldwych buses.

British Rail   Trains to Charing Cross Station; Strand approx. 500 yards to west end of Aldwych, left into Catherine Street, theatre on right 2 blocks along at corner of Russell Street.

THEATRE ROYAL, HAYMARKET

Haymarket SW1Y 4HT
Map refs: SF 140 F12, A-Z 60d D4
Box Office: 930 9832 (10am-8pm Mon-Sat)
Credit card booking: 930 9832
Stage door: 930 8890

Mainstream (plays)/traditional auditorium/proscenium stage/capacity 906/view ***/audibility ***/a-c **/heat **/ disabled facilities: contact box office/snacks/three bars/ performances: 7.30pm Mon-Sat + 2.30pm Wed and Sat.

Directly across the street from the gloriously neo-Baroque Her Majesty's Theatre stands the wonderful (and authentic) Georgian Theatre Royal, a masterpiece of architectural grace designed in 1821 by John Nash, it shares with the Drury Lane the distinction of being the only pre-Victorian 'period' theatre in London which is actually of its period. The Haymarket's history, as correct as its architecture, has long been distinguished by outstanding productions of both classical revivals and new works, a policy which continues to the present day.

BOOKING

£6.50-£13.50/concessions: contact box office/telephone booking: pay within three days of making reservation/ postal booking: cheques to 'Theatre Royal, Haymarket', include SAE/credit cards: Visa-Barclaycard, Access-Mastercard, Diners' Club, American Express.

GETTING THERE

buses 3, 6, 9, 12, 13, 14, 15, 19, 22, 23, 38, 53, 55, 88, 159 to Piccadilly Circus (or any stop in Haymarket); walk down Haymarket approx. 250 yards, theatre on left. 1, 24, 29, 77, 77A, 170, 172, 176 to Trafalgar Square; Pall Mall East, right into Haymarket, theatre on right a few yards along.

underground *Bakerloo Line, Piccadilly Line* to Piccadilly Circus; Haymarket exit, walk down Haymarket approx. 250 yards, theatre on left.

British Rail Trains to Charing Cross Station; Strand exit to Trafalgar Square, continue as for Trafalgar Square buses.

THEATRE ROYAL, STRATFORD EAST

Gerry Raffles Square, Stratford, E15 1BN
Map refs: SF 51 X19, A-Z 49 E2
Box Office: 534 0310 (10am-7pm)
Administration: 534 7374

Fringe (plays)/traditional auditorium/proscenium stage/ capacity 467/view ***/audibility ***/a-c: none/heat ***/ wheelchair access/snacks/one bar/extras: Sunday variety shows, children's theatre workshops/performances: 8pm Mon-Sat.

Built in 1884 and altered in 1902 by Frank Matcham, the Stratford Theatre Royal, now a protected building, stands like a small, rather tarnished Victorian bauble in the midst of post-war development in East London's Stratford New Town. Originally a suburban theatre devoted largely to popular comedies, farces, musicals and melodrama, the Stratford suddenly came to national prominence in 1963 when actress-manager Joan Littlewood installed her famous Theatre Workshop here and began staging major experimental productions of both classical and modern works which culminated in the triumphant black comedy-musical *Oh, What A Lovely War* in 1963. Since then the theatre has maintained a reputation for staging productions of the highest quality, though its policy has now been expanded to include lighter, family entertainment along with the modern, controversial works that are its mainstay.

BOOKING

£1.00-£6.00/concessions: OAPs, students, unemployed £1.00/telephone booking: collect-pay 1 hour before performance/postal booking: cheques to 'Theatre Royal', include SAE or collect at box office/credit cards: Visa-Barclaycard.

GETTING THERE

buses 10, 23, 69, 86, 108, 158, 173, 225, 238, 241, 262, 278, S1 to Stratford Station; walk up Great East Road following signs to theatre. Three minutes walk and theatre is on right. Posting to theatre.

underground *Central Line* to Stratford; directions as for Stratford buses.

British Rail Trains to Stratford; directions as for Stratford buses.

TRICYCLE THEATRE

269 Kilburn High Road NW6 7JR
Map refs: SF 45 V20, A-Z 43 E2
Box Office: 328 8626 (10am-8pm)
Information: 328 8626

Fringe (plays,)/2-tier gallery seating around 3 sides/ proscenium thrust stage/capacity 200/view ***/ audibility ***/a-c **/heat ***/disabled seating, hearing loops, adapted rest rooms (notify management in advance)/one restaurant/one bar/extras: young people and children's theatre workshops, art gallery/ performances: 8pm Mon-Sat, 4pm Sat (variable) 11.30 Sat (children's shows).

Opened in 1980 in a renovated dance hall, the Tricycle serves as home both for the Tricycle Company and for touring groups, staging 2-to-6-week runs of revivals, new plays and experimental works, along with regular Saturday programmes of children's theatre. From the most modest of beginnings, the Tricycle has now become one of London's important small fringe theatres.

BOOKING

£3.00-£5.50/concessions: OAPs, students, unemployed/ telephone booking: pay within three working days of making reservation/postal booking: cheques to 'Tricycle Theatre', include SAE or collect at door/credit cards: Visa-Barclaycard, Access-Mastercard.

GETTING THERE

buses 8, 16, 32, 176, 616 to Brondesbury Station; theatre a few yards south of station in Kilburn High Road.

underground *Jubilee Line* to Kilburn; right out of station, walk down Kilburn High Road approx. 400 yards, theatre on right just past Brondesbury Station.

British Rail Trains to Brondesbury Station; right out of station, theatre a few yards along in Kilburn High Road.

VAUDEVILLE THEATRE

404 Strand WC2R 0NH
Map refs: SF 140 L10, A-Z 60d A4
Box Office: 836 9987 (10am-8pm)
Credit card booking: as above
Stage door: 836 3191

Mainstream (plays, musicals)/traditional auditorium/ proscenium stage/capacity 694/view ***/audibility ***/ a-c ***/heat ***/wheelchair access/snacks/coffee-bar/three bars/performances: 8pm Mon-Fri, 2.30pm Wed, 5.00pm & 8.30pm Sat.

Built in 1870, this is one of London's most agreeable theatres, with its handsome neo-Georgian façade (added in 1891) and comfortable 'neo-Adam' interior, created by Atkinson in 1926, the Vaudeville has been associated through most of its history with consistently successful comedy and light drama. The enormously popular *Salad Days* played 2283 performances here starting in 1954, and more recent successes include Joyce Rayburn's *The Man Most Likely To*....and a marvellous version of Noel Coward's *Present Laughter*.

BOOKING

£5.00-£12.50/concessions: contact box office/telephone booking: pay within four days of making reservation/ postal booking: cheques to 'Vaudeville Theatre' include

SAE/credit cards: Visa-Barclaycard, Access-Mastercard, Diners' Club, American Express.

GETTING THERE

buses 1, 6, 9, 11, 13, 15, 23, 77, 77A, 170, 172, 176 to Strand, nearest stop to Southampton Street; theatre on north side of Strand approx. opposite the Savoy Hotel. 4, 5, 171, 188, 501, 502, 513 to Aldwych; walk in Strand toward Trafalgar Square, theatre on right approx. 200 yards along. 3, 12, 24, 29, 53, 88, 159 to Trafalgar Square; walk approx. 600 yards along Strand, theatre on left.

underground *Piccadilly Line* to Covent Garden; walk through market into Strand via Southampton St, then turn right. *Bakerloo Line, Jubilee Line, Northern Line* to Charing Cross Station; Strand exit, turn right into Strand and continue as for Trafalgar Square buses. *District or Circle Line* to Embankment; Villiers Street exit, walk up Villiers Street (away from river), right into Strand, continue as for Trafalgar Square buses.

British Rail Charing Cross Station; directions as for Charing Cross underground.

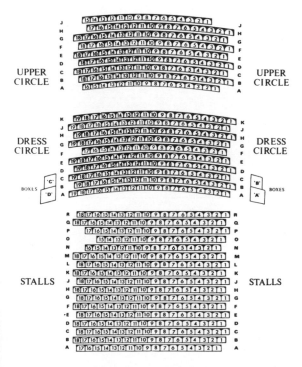

VICTORIA PALACE THEATRE

Victoria Street SW1E 5EA
Map refs: SF 147 Z 2-3, A-Z 62c B3
Box Office: 834 1317 (9am-9pm Mon-Sat)
Credit card booking: 828 4735, 828 4736
Stage door: 834 2781

Mainstream (musicals, variety, revue, plays, concerts)/
traditional auditorium/proscenium stage/capacity 1565/
view ***/audibility ***/a-c */heat ***/wheelchair access
(notify management in advance)/five bars/performance
times vary with productions: see press.

The Victoria Palace, with its neo-classical façade, huge
arched entrance and baroque tower, was built as a variety
hall by Frank Matcham in 1911 to replace the Old Royal
Standard Music Hall, demolished during the building of
Victoria Station. The new theatre continued to operate as a
music hall until the mid-1930s when policy shifted to plays
and musicals. The Black and White Minstrels brought old-
time revue entertainment back for an eight-year run
starting in 1962, and the theatre has since staged a
successful revival of *The Sound of Music*.

BOOKING

Telephone booking: pay within three days of making
reservation/postal booking: cheques to 'Victoria Palace

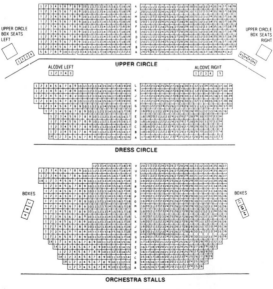

Theatre', include SAE/credit cards: Visa-Barclaycard, Access-Mastercard, American Express.

GETTING THERE

buses 2, 2B, 10, 11, 16, 24, 25, 29, 36, 36A, 36B, 38, 39, 52, 52A 55, 70, 76, 149, 185, 500, 507 to Victoria Station; walk directly away from main entrance to station, theatre in front of you near intersection of Victoria Street and Buckingham Palace Road.

underground *District or Circle Line* to Victoria Station; *or Victoria Line* to station main entrance and continue as for Victoria buses.

British Rail *Victoria Station*; to main station entrance and continue as for Victoria buses.

WAREHOUSE THEATRE, CROYDON

62 Dingwall Road, Croydon CR0 2NE
Map refs: SF 157 02, A-Z 118 C1
Box Office: 680 4060 (10am-8pm Mon-Sat, 3pm-8pm Sun)

Fringe (plays)/studio seating (raked)/flexible, open acting area/capacity 100-120/view ***/audibility ***/a-c: none/heat **/disabled facilities: none/one bar, hot and cold snacks available/extras: Sat morning children's shows, theatre workshops, cabaret and art exhibitions/performances: 8pm Tues-Sat, 5pm Sun.

Founded in 1977 as a lunchtime venue, The Warehouse has now gone over to evening performances (plus a Sunday matinée), featuring small-scale theatre committed to new writing and occasional revivals of classics, with audiences drawn from all over London.

WAREHOUSE THEATRE . R.Ab.

BOOKING

£2.00-£4.50/concessions: students, OAPs, unemployed/telephone booking: pay three days before performance if possible (but half hour before is OK)/postal booking: contact Box Office/credit cards: none/membership required—reciprocal with other fringe theatres.

GETTING THERE

buses 12A, 50, 54, 60, 64, 68, 75, 109, 119, 119B, 130, 130B, 154, 157, 166, 166A, 190, 194, 194B, 197, 213, 289 to East Croydon Station or nearest bus-stop; theatre is signposted at intersection of George Street and Dingwall Road, adjacent to station. One-minute walk to theatre.

British Rail to East Croydon Station (15min from Victoria, 10 min from Clapham Junction), then as above.

WESTMINSTER THEATRE

Palace Street SW1E 5JB
Map refs: SF 148 B2, A-Z 62c B2
Box Office: 834 0283, 834 0284 (10am-8pm Mon-Sat)
Credit card booking: 834 0048
Stage door: 834 7882

Mainstream (plays, musicals, pantomime)/traditional auditorium/proscenium stage/capacity 600/view ***/audibility ***/a-c: none/heat ***/wheelchair access, hearing loops (notify management in advance)/one restaurant/one snack-bar/extra: bookshop/performances: 7.45pm Mon-Sat, 2.30pm Wed & Sat/Children's shows: 10.30pm & 2pm Mon-Thurs, 2.30pm & 6pm Fri-Sat.

Opened in 1931 in a converted wayfarers' chapel near Victoria Station, the Westminster showed great early promise as a serious theatre, staging Pirandello, Eugene O'Neill, Shaw, Ibsen and Granville-Barker under Anmer Hall's management, before becoming the home, until 1939, of J.B. Priestley's Mask Theatre. Moral Rearmament staged productions here between 1946 and 1949, and continued to run the theatre for independent companies until quite recently. In 1982 the Westminster earned the distinction of being the only London theatre in history to stage a play written by a Pope—*The Jeweller's Shop* by John Paul II.

BOOKING

£4.00-£8.00/concessions: contact box office/telephone booking: pay within three working days of making reservation/postal booking: cheques to 'Westminster Theatre', include SAE/credit cards: Visa-Barclaycard, Access-Mastercard, American Express.

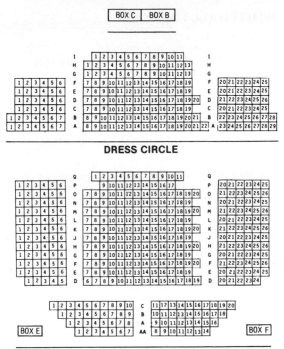

DRESS CIRCLE

STALLS

STAGE

GETTING THERE

buses 2, 2B, 10, 11, 16, 24, 25, 29, 36, 36B, 38, 39, 52, 52A, 55, 70, 76, 149, 185, 500, 507 to Victoria Station (or nearest stop); to Victoria Street (the big main street on your left as you face Victoria station entrance), left into Palace Street, theatre on right.

underground *District or Circle Line, Victoria Line* to Victoria Station; directions as for Victoria buses.

British Rail to Victoria Station; directions as for Victoria buses.

WHITEHALL THEATRE

14 Whitehall SW1A 2DY
Map refs: SF 140 H-J14, A-Z 60d D-E4
Box Office: 930 7765, 839 4455 (10am-8pm Mon-Sat)
Credit card bookings: 379 6565, 379 6433
Group Booking: 836 3962
Stage Door: 930 0988

Mainstream (plays, comedies)/traditional auditorium/
proscenium stage/capacity 620/view ***/audibility ***/
a-c ***/heat ***/help is available to carry disabled to seating
in Royal Circle (notify management in advance)/Whitehall
Café-Bar in foyer open from 12 noon/spacious stalls bars/
Ticketmaster desk in foyer selling tickets for most
theatres, concerts and sports events in London, open
10am-8pm/performance times vary: check with Box Office
or see press.

Opened in 1930 by actor-manager Walter Hackett as a
West End home for light comedies, the Whitehall became
a striptease house during World War II and then, in 1950,
came into its own as one of London's leading theatres
when Brian Rix began staging a series of topical farces felt
by many critics to rival the famous 'Aldwych Farces' of the
1920's, and '30's. Farce continued to hold sway through
the 1960's, but in 1969 exotic entertainments impresario
Paul Raymond assumed management of the theatre,
shifted to his own favourite policy, and opened with a
nude version of *Pyjama Tops*. Comedy reappeared briefly
in 1981, but in 1983, with the outbreak of the Falklands
conflict, the theatre was transformed into a war museum.
In 1985 the theatre was bought by the Maybox Group (who
also own the Albery, Criterion, Donmar Warehouse,
Piccadilly and Wyndham's Theatres), and after a one-
million-pound refurbishment was opened in the Spring of
1986. It has been restored to its original Art Deco
splendour and with the added improvements is now one
of the most comfortable theatres in London.

BOOKING

Concessions: OAPs, students, unemployed, Registered
Deaf or Blind, under-24 Rail Card holders (all standby
tickets), groups of 12 or more/telephone booking: pay
within three days of making reservation/postal booking:
cheques to 'Whitehall Theatre ', include SAE/credit cards:
Visa-Barclaycard, Access-Mastercard, Diners' Club,
American Express.

GETTING THERE

buses 3, 11, 12, 24, 29, 53, 77, 77A, 88, 159, 170, 172 to
Whitehall (nearest stop to Strand); theatre on west side of
Whitehall, south side of Trafalgar Square. 1, 6, 9, 13, 15,
23, 176 to Trafalgar Square; to bottom of Trafalgar Square,
cross Strand, theatre on right a few yards down Whitehall.

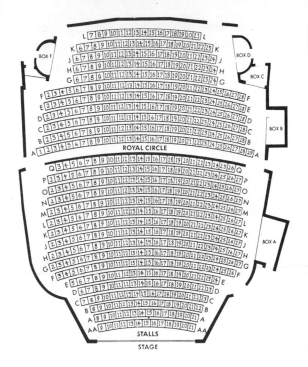

underground *Bakerloo Line, Jubilee Line, Northern Line* to Charing Cross Station; The Mall exit, cross The Mall by Admiralty Arch, theatre a few yards down on right. *District or Circle Line* to Westminster; Whitehall exit, walk uphill in Whitehall approx 600 yards, theatre on left.

British Rail Trains to Charing Cross Station; directions as for Charing Cross underground.

WIMBLEDON THEATRE

The Broadway, Wimbledon SW19 1QG
Map refs: SF 105 X16-17, A-Z 105 E1
Box Office: 540 0362, 540 0363 (10am-8pm daily—Sept-April)
Stage Door: 542 1333

Mainstream (plays, musicals, opera, ballet, concerts)/traditional auditorium/proscenium stage/capacity 1700/view ***/audibility ***/a-c (theatre closed May-August)/heat ***/wheelchair access (notify management in advance)/hearing loops/snacks/five bars/performances: seven evening and two matinée performances per week during season. Times and dates vary according to the production; contact Box Office for details.

Most notable architecturally for its open-work, wrought-iron circle and balcony railings, the neo-classical Wimbledon Theatre opened in 1910 as a community theatre staging mainly comedies and drama for local audiences. Owned by the local borough council and, since 1980, leased to commercial management, the theatre has expanded its policy and is now used for a variety of theatrical and related activities, including touring and pre-West End productions.

BOOKING

£3.00-£6.50/OAPs, children, parties of 20 or more/telephone booking: pay within 4 days of making reservation/postal booking: cheques to 'Wimbledon Theatre', include SAE or collect at Box Office/credit cards: Visa-Barclaycard, Access-Mastercard.

GETTING THERE

buses 57, 80, 93, 131, 155 to The Broadway, (ask for Wimbledon Theatre or Russell Road); theatre at corner of Russell Road and The Broadway. 77A, 156, 200 to Wimbledon Station; walk down the Broadway to Russell Road, theatre on right.

underground *District Line* to Wimbledon Station; directions as for Wimbledon Station buses.

British Rail Wimbledon Station; directions as for Wimbledon Station buses.

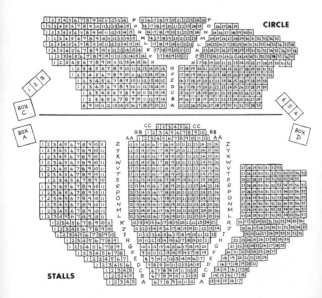

144

WYNDHAM'S THEATRE

Charing Cross Road WC2H 0DA
Map refs: SF 140 9H, A-Z 60d E3
Box Office: 836 3028 (10am-8pm Mon-Sat)
Credit card booking: 379 6565, 379 6433
Group booking: 836 3962
Stage Door: 836 5650

Mainstream (plays, musicals)/traditional auditorium/
proscenium stage/capacity 760/view ***/audibility ***/a-c*/
heat **/disabled seating/infra-red hearing facilities (notify
management in advance)/snacks/three bars/performance
times vary with productions: see press.

Built for actor-manager Sir Charles Wyndham in 1899 by
the renowned Victorian theatre designer W.G.R.
Sprague, Wyndham's is one of London's most strikingly
attractive smaller theatres, its interior a triumph of neo-
Georgian decorative invention, its façade a handsome
evocation of the Italian Renaissance. Formerly run by

145

England's leading theatrical management family, the Alberys, Wyndham's maintains a reputation, rare in the West End, for staging works of only the highest calibre, be they dramas, comedies or musicals. The theatre also maintains a close association with the fringe through its proprietorship of the Donmar Warehouse. Among the critically and popularly acclaimed works that have been staged here since World War II are *The Hostage*, *Oh, What A Lovely War*, *The Miracle Worker*, *The Prime Of Miss Jean Brodie*, *The Boys In The Band* and *No Man's Land*.

BOOKING

Concessions: OAPs, students, unemployed, Registered Deaf or blind, under-24 British Rail cardholders (all standby tickets), group of 12 or more/telephone booking: pay within three days of making reservation/postal booking: cheques to 'Wyndham's Theatre', include SAE/ credit cards: Visa-Barclaycard, Access-Mastercard, Diners' Club, American Express.

GETTING THERE

buses 1, 24, 29, 176, N90 to Leicester Square; theatre visible at Charing Cross Road and Cranbourn Street. 3, 6, 9, 11, 12, 13, 15, 53, 77, 77A, 88, 159, 170, 172 to Trafalgar Square; walk uphill through St. Martin's Place (keeping National Gallery, National Portrait Gallery on left),

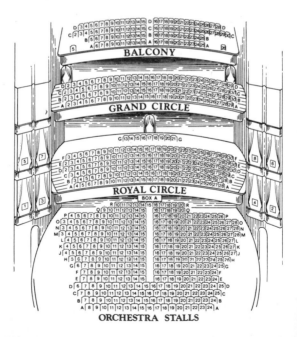

continue on into Charing Cross Road, theatre approx. 400 yards on right. 14, 19, 22, 38, 55 to Cambridge Circus; walk downhill in Charing Cross Road approx. 300 yards, theatre on left.

underground *Northern Line, Piccadilly Line* to Leicester Square; theatre visible from all Charing Cross Road exits at Charing Cross Road and Cranbourn Street. *Bakerloo Line, Jubilee Line* to Charing Cross Station; *Bakerloo Line, Jubilee Line*/Strand exit to Trafalgar Square, continue as for Trafalgar Square buses. *Central Line* to Tottenham Court Road; walk downhill in Charing Cross Road approx. 500 yards, theatre on left.

British Rail Charing Cross Station; directions as for Charing Cross underground.

YAA ASANTEWA ARTS CENTRE

1 Chippenham Mews W9 2AN
Map refs: SF 129 U19, A-A 59 F1
Box Office: 286 1656

Fringe (plays, performance)/two auditoria, both with flexible seating/open acting areas/view ***/audibility ***/ a-c: none/heat **/main theatre: capacity 200, with disabled facilities/first-floor theatre: capacity 80, no disabled facilities/one buffet bar, one bar shared with Arts Centre/ performances: 7.30pm Thurs-Sat.

Formerly The Factory, this spacious building with two theatre areas was reopened in 1976 as an arts centre for the multi-ethnic population in the Westminster area, and has developed into a leading venue for Black Arts. It hosts a wide variety of daytime and evening activities including dance, drama, music etc. Most theatrical productions take place in the first-floor theatre.

BOOKING

£2.00-£2.50/concessions: OAPs, students, unemployed, arts centre members/telephone booking: collect and pay 30 minutes before performance/postal booking: none/ credit cards: none.

GETTING THERE

buses 18, 28, 31, 36, or 36B to Prince of Wales; walk to Elgin Avenue, right into Athens Gardens, continue across Chippenham Road into Chippenham Mews.

underground *Metropolitan Line* to Westbourne Park; turn left out of station, walk up Great Western Road, across canal, right into Woodfield Road, along to Harrow Road then across to Chippenham Road and right into Chippenham Mews.

British Rail to Westbourne Park, then directions as above.

YOUNG VIC

66 The Cut, Waterloo SE1 8LP
Map refs: SF 141 U-V 16-17, A-Z 63a B1
Box Office: 928 6363 (10am-8pm Mon-Sat)
Credit card booking: 379 6433 (Ticketmaster)

Main theatre Fringe (plays, musicals)/fixed raked seating on three sides/platform end stage/capacity 450/view ***/audibility ***/a-c **/heat **/wheelchair access (notify management in advance).

Studio theatre Fringe (plays, performance)/flexible raked seating/platform stage/capacity 120/view ***/audibility ***/a-c **/heat **/wheelchair access (notify management in advance).

both theatres One buffet-wine-coffee bar/one bar/performances: 7.30pm Mon-Sat + 2pm Wed and Fri.

Founded in 1970 as a branch of the National Theatre Company, and housed in a converted Victorian butcher's shop a few yards away from the Old Vic, the Young Vic maintains a lively policy of mounting professional repertory productions designed for both young and adult audiences, with the Young Vic Company holding forth in the main theatre and the studio given over to touring groups. Frank Dunlop and Michael Bogdanov have both been directors of the Young Vic in the past, and while the theatre lives permanently on or near the financial brink, it still manages admirably to go on staging some of the finest productions to be seen in London today.

BOOKING

£3.50-£5.95/concessions: OAPs, students, children, unemployed, disabled, groups of 10+/telephone booking: pay within seven days of making reservation/postal booking: cheques to 'Young Vic', with SAE/credit cards: Visa-Barclaycard, Access-Mastercard, Diners' Club, American Express (if tel. booking through Ticketmaster); no credit cards accepted at Box Office.

GETTING THERE

buses 1, 4, 5, 68, 70, 76, 149, 171, 176, 177, 188, 501, 502, 507, 513 to Waterloo Station; turn right out of station, walk down Waterloo Road, turn left into The Cut, theatre on left a few yards along.

Underground *Bakerloo or Northern Line* to Waterloo; directions as above.

British Rail Trains to Waterloo, then as above.

SECTION III
GLOSSARY OF THEATRE TERMS

III GLOSSARY OF THEATRE TERMS

Act Formal division of a play into one or more scenes. First introduced to English theatre by Ben Jonson in the late 16th-century. (Scholars believe Shakespeare's plays were not divided into acts in their original versions). In pre-modern playwrighting, tragedies where divided into five acts, comedies into three or four. Today nearly all plays are written in two acts.

Action (1) In a play script: any specific objective a character must accomplish. (2) The sequence of events in a play.

Alternative theatre General term for a theatre or theatrical company which does not deal in mainstream productions. Fringe theatre, experimental theatre, cabaret, revue etc. are all forms of alternative theatre.

Apron Portion of a stage which extends toward the audience beyond the proscenium arch. Before the 19th-century, the apron thrust several yards beyond the proscenium and served as the main acting area. Victorian theatre designers reduced its size to the now familiar depth of three or four feet.

Arena In English stage design, an open platform stage built at one end of an auditorium, with seating on three sides. In US design, the central acting area in a theatre-in-the-round.

Backdrop (Also Backcloth). A flat, unframed canvas hung across the back of the stage on which scenes may be painted.

Benefit A play or other entertainment staged to raise money for a worthy cause—often needy actors or their families.

Boards Colloquial for 'the stage'.

Box Set A stage set, usually built with flats, which represents a complete room—walls, doors, windows, sometimes even a ceiling.

Burlesque Originally, a satire which parodied a currently popular dramatic fashion or particular play (18th-century). Now, any broadly satirical parody. The US meaning of striptease is not used in the English theatre.

Business (1) Theatrical term for any repeated gesture, mannerism, voice inflection, etc. used by an actor to enhance the individuality or believability of a character he or she is playing; also to focus audience attention on the character. (2) Interplay between (usually) two actors during exchange of dialogue, completion of an action, etc. aimed at bringing some special or added quality to the moment; normally of the actors' own devising rather than the director's. (3) Colloquial for the entertainment profession in general; show business.

Cabaret An intimate revue, usually staged in a club or restaurant, involving a few players performing songs and sketches, often based on a topical theme.

Call (1) A notice posted backstage on a call board informing actors of rehearsal schedules, auditions, cast changes, etc. (2) An announcement telling actors when they are next expected on stage.

Cellar Area directly below the stage housing machinery for scene changing, special effects, traps etc.

Chorus Originally a group of performers in Greek drama who commented upon the main action of a play without participating in it. Now, a group of dancers or singers who perform ensemble in musical productions.

Church drama Modern version of the liturgical drama popular in Medieval English theatre. T.S. Eliot's *Murder in the Cathedral* is a typical example.

Claque Group of hired spectators paid by the theatre management to applaud enthusiastically in an audience.

Closet drama A play written specifically to be read aloud rather than performed.

Cloth General for an expanse of painted canvas used on stage as scenery.

Comedy Originally, a satire. Later, the opposite of tradedy; any play in which the central conflict is happily resolved. Today, comedy refers to any play whose conflict or situation is itself amusing or lighthearted as opposed to serious.

Command performance A play or other stage entertainment presented at the express request of the monarch.

Cue A word, gesture, or other piece of business delivered on stage which serves as a signal for another actor's next speech, action, entry, exit, etc.

Curtain Properly, the front-curtain or house curtain, hung just behind the proscenium arch, which is raised and lowered between acts of a play.

Cyclorama A rigid, seamless wall of plaster or canvas curving around the back and sides of the stage on which sky and cloud effects can be created with light projections.

Dame Pantomime dame: traditional female character in English pantomime, always played by a man.

Dark Theatrical term designating a day or longer time period when a theatre is closed.

Director (1) Person responsible for the interpretation of a play and for overseeing rehearsals. (2) Creative head of a theatrical company, responsible for choosing dramatic material, hiring actors, arranging the repertoire etc. Also in some cases, the administrator of the company's home theatre.

Domestic comedy Any comedy in which the main conflict or situation centres upon family matters.

Downstage Stage direction indicating the front of the stage; the area nearest the audience.

Drag Colloquial for cross-dressing. An actor costumed in women's clothes or an actress costumed in men's.

Drama (1) General term for any play with mainly spoken dialogue (2) A play who's development involves a serious conflict between two or more characters. (3)The opposite of comedy: a serious as opposed to a funny play.

Dress Circle The raked tier of seats located directly above the orchestra stalls in a theatre. The term 'dress' derives from the 19th-century practise of wearing formal clothes when taking seats in the first circle.

Drop Short for backcloth or backdrop.

Entr'acte An entertainment, usually musical, between the acts of a play.

Equity Short for British Actors' Equity Association, the trade union to which all professional actors in Britain belong.

Expressionism A school of playwrighting which seeks to dramatize psychological facts and conflicts rather than material ones.

Farce A branch of comedy which relies for its effects largely upon stereotype characters involved in elaborately contrived situations. Farce also designates any broad, knock-about comedy. The Aldwych theatre was famous for its farces in the 1920s and 30s, as was the Whitehall theatre just after World War II.

Feed Colloquial for delivering a line of dialogue.

Feed line A straight line (US). Any line of dialogue delivered for the sole purpose of setting up a comic response.

Flat Canvas stretched tightly over a wooden frame and used as a basic element of stage scenery to create walls, partitions and the like.

Footlights A line of small flood lights hidden in traps along the front edge of the stage which provide general lighting from below.

Fourth wall A dramatic convention which treats the empty plane of space outlined by the proscenium arch as if it were a real wall in a room.

Fringe A general term for any experimental or otherwise unconventional dramatic work; also general for theatres which regularly stage such works. The term was first applied to small, experimental works staged independently at the annual Edinburgh International Festival of Music and Drama in the early 1960s. Roughly equivalent to the US term 'off-Broadway'

Gallery   The top balcony of a theatre.

Gods, The   Colloquial for a theatre balcony, so-called because of its proximity to the ceiling where decoration frequently features plaster angels and cherubs.

House   Theatrical term for both a theatre and a theatre audience. 'Front of house' or simply 'front' is the theatre auditorium.

Interlude   A dramatic sketch or short play, usually containing comic elements or characters, and dealing mainly with earthly rather than universal subjects. The form became popular in England after 1500 and is generally agreed by scholars to represent the bridge between older Medieval religious drama and the theatre of Shakespeare and his contemporaries.

Kitchen Sink   Colloquial for a school of realistic, contemporary playwrighting which dealt largely the with material and psychological problems of young working class men and women in England of the 1950s and 60s. Bleak, angry, and unglamourous, the Kitchen Sink offended a great number of people (on the whole intentionally) but it also produced some of England's best modern playwrights, among them John Osborne, David Storey and Arnold Wesker.

Limelight   Colloquially, a bright light illuminating celebrity; the centre of attention. Originally, a 19th century stage lighting technique in which a lime or calcium flare, which produces dazzling white light, was ignited off-stage to create the effect of sun—or moonlight shining into a scene.

Lunch-time theatre   A new form of theatre, begun in London during the 1960s, in which short, usually experimental plays are performed to small audiences in pubs, wine bars, bistros, restaurants and the like during the lunch hour.

Mainstream   A general term for any conventional play or other dramatic stage entertainment; also general for theatres which regularly stage such works. Used descriptively in opposition to 'fringe'.

Manager   Originally, the person responsible for all financial aspects of staging a theatrical production. Now, the administrative executive of a theatre.

Matinée   A daytime or early evening performance in the theatre.

Melodrama   Originally, a spoken passage in an opera accompanied by music. Now, a drama which deals in sensation, deliberately exaggerated emotion, and clichéd notions of good and evil.

Method   A school of acting, adapted from Stanislavsky's teaching at the Moscow Art Theatre in the early 20th century, in which an actor seeks to 'lose' himself in the character he is playing by applying appropriate emotions remembered from his own past to conflicts and events that arise in the character's fictional life.

Musical comedy A play, usually lighthearted in tone (though not necessarily), which incorporates song and usually dance as integral parts of the narrative. Evolved from 19th-century operetta.

Music Hall (1) Variety entertainment, popular in 19th and early 20th century England, which features comic turns, singers, acrobats, jugglers, and sometimes short scenes from serious dramas. Roughly the British equivalent of U.S. Vaudeville. (2) A theatre that stages variety entertainment.

National Theatre England's first state-supported theatrical repertory company, founded in 1962 with Sir Laurence Olivier as its director, and housed since 1976 in its permanent London home in the South Bank complex where it has 3 theatres of widely differing design at its disposal. The company, numbering some 600 creative, administrative and technical personnel, produces 20 to 30 plays every season, mixing classics, modern revivals, musicals and experimental works, and presenting limited runs of each two or three times during the year. Acting personnel changes from one year to the next, but in any season at least a dozen of England's finest and most celebrated actors and actresses will be found playing with the National in a variety of leading roles.

One/in one Theatrical term for appearing on stage alone. Hamlet's soliloquy, for example, is delivered 'in one'.

Open stage A raised, platform stage built without proscenium arch or side walls at one end of a theatre auditorium.

Operetta A comic or light opera. 19-century forerunner of the modern musical comedy.

Orchestra The ground-level seats in a theatre auditorium; the stalls.

Pantomime A traditional English Christmas entertainment, always based on some children's fairy tale— Sleeping Beauty, Bluebeard, Jack and the Beanstalk—but expanded into a spectacular romantic farce with the addition of popular songs, slapstick comedy routines, acrobatics, and all sorts of specialty acts. Invariably featured in the cast are a young hero, the Principal Boy, who is always played by a girl, and a comic old woman, the Pantomime Dame, who is always played by a man.

Pit (1) In Elizabethan times, the floor of a theatre where spectators stood to watch performances. (2) The area directly in front of a stage and several feet below stage level where musicians can perform without blocking the audience's view of the actors.

Producer Person responsible for all financial aspects of staging a theatrical production.

Prologue A speech or poem delivered by a member of the cast before the action of a play begins. Used to set the scene, describe important events that occurred before the time of the play's action, or to present the author's comments on what will follow.

Prompter Theatrical crew member responsible for feeding forgotten lines or cues to actors on stage. The prompter sits just out of sight in the wings or concealed in a prompter's box, following the play's progress in a marked-up copy of the script called a prompt book.

Proscenium arch An arch standing at the front of the stage through which the audience views the action of a play as if looking through a picture frame or window. First introduced in Italy in 1618, the proscenium stage revolutionized the interior design of English theatres after 1660 and has only recently begun to go out of fashion with a return to popularity of the more flexible open plan stage.

Provinces Theatrical term for any location outside of a major city. In England, actors tend to use the term in reference to any theatre town, however large or small, which is not London.

Rake The angle of slope of a stage floor or section of theatre seats.

Repertory The collection of plays chosen for production each season by a theatrical repertory company.

Repertory company A permanent company of actors and actresses who select and prepare several plays at once and present them in a regularly rotating programme, giving a limited run to each. Some rep. companies work only in a single home theatre, others perform exclusively on tour, many divide their time between home and the road, and a few, like the National and the RSC, are large enough to make up several companies and do both simultaneously.

Returns Paid tickets for a performance which have been returned to the box office for resale.

Revival A play or other dramatic work which is brought back to the stage subsequent to the close of its first run.

Revue A stage entertainment featuring a mixture of short dramatic sketches, songs and sometimes dance, unified by a topical or satirical theme.

RSC The Royal Shakespeare Company; together with the National the largest and most prestigious of England's subsidized theatrical repertory companies, founded at Stratford-upon-Avon in 1960 by Sir Peter Hall and resident in various London theatres including the Aldwych, Roundhouse and Donmar Warehouse until 1982 when it moved to its permanent home at the Barbican.

Run Theatrical term for the number of continuous performances a play is given from its opening night to its closing.

Safety Curtain A fireproof curtain sometimes iron, which can be lowered behind the proscenium arch to separate the audience from the stage in the event of fire.

Scene (1) one complete passage of continuous action in a play. (2) The complete visual setting of part or all of a play; the set. (3) The background circumstances – time, location, prevailing historical, political, personal or other conditions – against which the action of a play unfolds.

Scenery All objects used on stage to represent the place where a play's action unfolds.

Set The complete decoration of the stage: scenery, plus furniture, plus all props not actually carried by the actors.

Sight line Technical term for the direct line of view from any seat in a theatre auditorium to various points around the stage; an essential consideration in theatre design.

Slips (1) Narrow openings in stage scenery through which actors may enter and exit. (2) A narrow row of seats located along the side walls of an auditorium.

Stage (1) The area where actors perform before an audience. A stage may be as simple as a clear space marked out on the ground or as complicated as the modern proscenium theatre stage. (2) General term for the acting profession and for all things theatrical.

Stage door Entry from the street to the backstage areas of a theatre.

Stage left Stage direction indicating the left hand side of the stage as seen from the audience.

Stage right Stage direction indicating the right hand side of the stage as seen from the audience.

Stalls The seats located on the floor of a theatre auditorium. Also orchestra stalls and (US) orchestra.

Stand-in An actor who temporarily replaces another in a role.

Stock company (1) A repertory company which performs a different play from its repertory each night. The name 'stock' derives from the fact that each principal player in the company specialized in a standard, or 'stock' role—the tragic hero, the ingénue, the clown, the foolish old woman, etc. (2) US term for a touring repertory company, espeically one which works during the Summer only.

Theatre-in-the-round A theatre designed with the stage at the centre of the auditorium and seating all the way around.

Theatre Club A theatre which is in principle run as a private club but which is in fact open to the public through the payment of a token membership fee. Theatre clubs were founded as a means óf circumventing restrictive censorship laws which continued to operate in England until 1968. Since then some smaller fringe theatres have maintained their club status in order to keep down license fees.

Thrust stage An apron stage; a stage which extends into the audience.

Tragedy (1) Properly, a drama dealing with some important theme in which the hero understands his predicament but cannot resolve it without condemning himself to profound loss or death, thereby becoming, in effect, the victim of his own fate. (2) Generally, any drama which ends with the hero's death.

Tragi-comedy A form of tragedy in which the larger circumstances surrounding the drama are happily resolved despite, or even because of, the hero's death. Also, a tragic drama which contains a number of comic elements, or one in which the hero himself is a pitiable or somewhat ridiculous figure rather than conventionally 'heroic'.

Understudy An actor in a company responsible for learning another actor's role so that he or she can go on as a replacement if circumstances demand.

Upstage (1) The back of the stage; the area furthest from the audience. (2) Colloquial for any trick played by an actor aimed at drawing the audience's attention away from another actor. The expression derives from the fact that the trick is usually played 'upstage' from the victim; ie. behind his back as he faces the audience.

Vaudeville US equivalent of English Music Hall.

Variety Alternative term for Music Hall.

Walk-on A very brief role in play, usually involving the delivery of no more than one line.

Well-made play A neatly organized, often superficial drama whose script makes thematic or literary sacrifices for the sake of mechanical cleverness.

Wings Unframed canvas drops or framed canvas flats placed obliquely at the sides of the stage as part of the scenery so that they appear as an unbroken surface from the audience but allow actors to enter and exit between them. Also, a general term for the area just off stage where actors wait to make their entrances.

LONDON'S

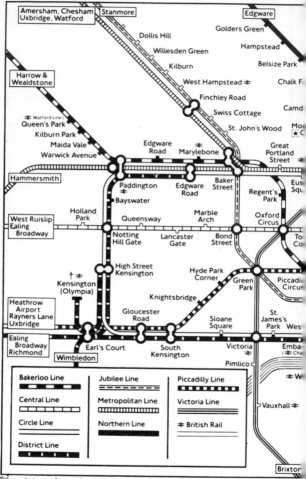

Amersham, Chesham, Uxbridge, Watford — Stanmore — Edgware

Golders Green
Dollis Hill
Hampstead
Willesden Green
Belsize Park
Kilburn
West Hampstead ≉ — Chalk F
Harrow & Wealdstone
Finchley Road
Camd
≉ Watford Line
Queen's Park — Swiss Cottage
Kilburn Park — St. John's Wood — Mor ★C
Maida Vale — Edgware Road — Marylebone — Great Portland Street ≉
Warwick Avenue
Hammersmith
Paddington — Edgware Road — Baker Street — Eus Squ
Bayswater — Regent's Park
West Ruislip Ealing Broadway
Holland Park — Queensway — Marble Arch — Oxford Circus — To Co
Notting Hill Gate — Lancaster Gate — Bond Street
High Street Kensington — Hyde Park Corner — Green Park — Piccadi Circus
† ≉ Kensington (Olympia)
Knightsbridge
Heathrow Airport Rayners Lane Uxbridge
Gloucester Road — Sloane Square — St. James's Park — West
Ealing Broadway Richmond
Earl's Court — South Kensington — Victoria ≉ — Emba ≉ Cha
Wimbledon
Pimlico ≉ W
≉ Vauxhall ≉
Brixtor

Bakerloo Line	Jubilee Line	Piccadilly Line
Central Line	Metropolitan Line	Victoria Line
Circle Line	Northern Line	≉ British Rail
District Line		

UNDERGROUND

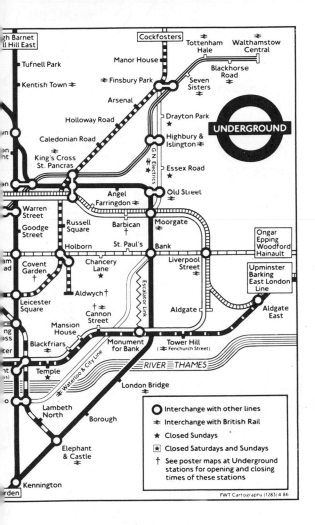

UNDERGROUND

O	Interchange with other lines	
⇌	Interchange with British Rail	
★	Closed Sundays	
🟊	Closed Saturdays and Sundays	
†	See poster maps at Underground stations for opening and closing times of these stations	

FWT Cartography (1283) 4 86

THE THEATRES OF

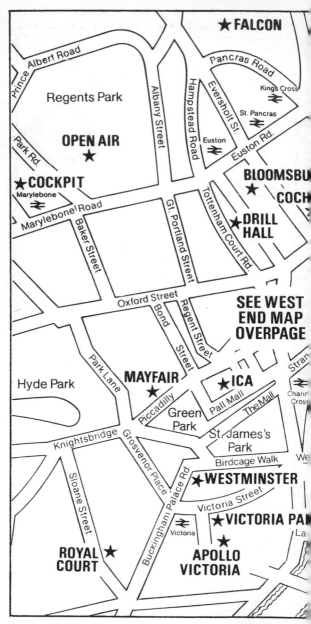

★ **FALCON**

Prince Albert Road

Pancras Road

Regents Park

Kings Cross

Albany Street

Hampstead Road

Eversholt St.

St. Pancras

Euston

Euston Rd.

OPEN AIR
★

Park Rd.

★ **COCKPIT**

Marylebone

BLOOMSBU
★

COCH

Marylebone Road

Baker Street

Gt. Portland Street

Tottenham Court Rd.

★ **DRILL
HALL**

Oxford Street

Bond Street

Regent Street

**SEE WEST
END MAP
OVERPAGE**

Park Lane

MAYFAIR
★

★ **ICA**

Stran

Hyde Park

Piccadilly

Green
Park

Pall Mall

The Mall

Charin
Cross

Knightsbridge

Grosvenor Place

St. James's
Park

Birdcage Walk

We

Sloane Street

Buckingham Palace Rd.

★ **WESTMINSTER**

Victoria Street

Victoria

★ **VICTORIA PA**

La

**ROYAL
COURT** ★

★
**APOLLO
VICTORIA**

CENTRAL LONDON

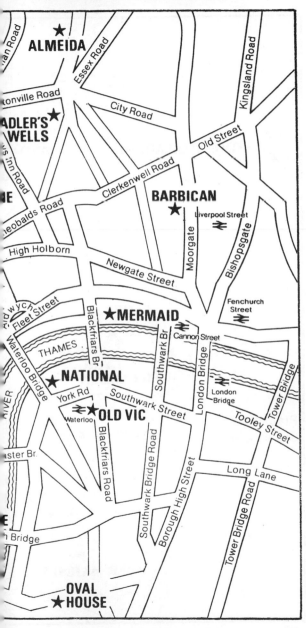

THE THEATRES OF

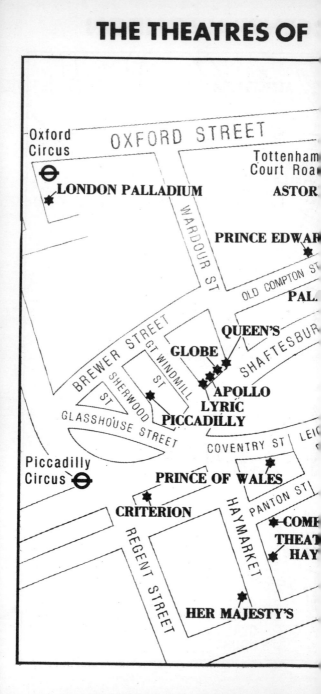

Oxford Circus

OXFORD STREET

Tottenham Court Road

LONDON PALLADIUM

ASTOR

WARDOUR ST

PRINCE EDWARD

OLD COMPTON ST

PAL

BREWER STREET

QUEEN'S

GLOBE

SHAFTESBUR

GT WINDMILL ST

SHERWOOD ST

APOLLO

LYRIC

GLASSHOUSE STREET

PICCADILLY

COVENTRY ST

LEIC

Piccadilly Circus

PRINCE OF WALES

PANTON ST

HAYMARKET

CRITERION

COMP
THEAT
HAY

REGENT STREET

HER MAJESTY'S